Unique
Golf Resorts
of the
World

UNIQUE GOLF RESORTS OF THE WORLD

Gwen Williams

Dedication

To the discriminating golfer
and discerning traveler who
admits to having an insatiable
appetite for the finest room
accommodations, service, and
food; who demands a "unique" golfing
experience and can accept
the best the world
has to offer.

ISBN 0-9612294-1-1
Library of Congress Catalog: 83-90911

Published by
Unique Golf Resorts of the World
4501 Camden Drive
Corona del Mar, California 92625
Printed in the United States of America

Contents

Contents

Contents

Contents

*The game of golf,
dated 1501.*

*Historians are not
agreed on the origins of
golf. Some date it from
12th Century Holland,
where a golf-like game
was played on ice.
However, over the past
500 years, it was the
Scots who developed and
popularized the game
after initially outlawing
it because it was taking
too much time from the
practice of archery,
deemed necessary for the
defense of the realm.*

As it used to be, on ice.

Introduction

For years as a golfing traveler and curiosity seeker, it was difficult for me to obtain adequate information regarding golf resorts that were the "ultimate" and would appeal to the discerning traveler. Through numerous disappointments, I was inspired to combine extensive travel and personal research in order to seek out the best the world has to offer.

As a golfer, my quest was not only for a championship calibre golf course, but for the finest in room accommodations, great food, impeccable service, and a total "golf resort" destination. We know it is rare to find the best golf course, the best hotel, and the best food and service at one resort, but proudly we present the finest we have found in the world—truly a "unique" combination of...

American Hurrahs...   Desert Oases...
Carribean Hideaways...   Mountain Retreats...
Dude Ranches...   Elegant Castles...
European Traditions...   Fashionable Health Spas...
Five-Star Hotels...   and more...

On the following pages you will be introduced to a number of resorts which have received recognition and awards. In each case, congratulations are in order as I, too, feel they have earned the recognition. Because a resort does not have a particular award, however, certainly does not discredit it in any way.

Careful screening and adherence to rigid standards in selecting each resort, plus personally visiting the greatest majority of them have been only part of the preparation for this book. Some statistics still had to be obtained from the resorts themselves. I have presented the facts to you as I have received them. In our world things rarely remain the same, and changes could occur even at this writing. However, should any changes take place, my prediction is that they would most likely be of a positive nature.

My sincere desire is that you, too, will feel an exuberant flair for life and a boundless delight in identifying with the passion and beauty of these most exciting golf resorts.

Now you can escape to a world that will open your eyes, touch your heart, and reach your soul...

Golfingly yours,
Gwen Williams

Gwen Williams

Gwen Williams, a ''UNIQUE'' combination of talent and experience is an enthusiastic golfer with a very respectable handicap.

For several years she has played team for her own private country club, as well as serving on many ladies' boards.

Her upbeat attitude, dynamic drive, and a quest for excellence has prompted her to expand and update her already best selling first edition.

Now you can take an arm chair tour and become acquainted with the ''latest'' and the ''greatest'' golf resorts in the world.

Gwen and her husband Harlan share the spirit of travel and a love of golf, and as a team, present this publication for your pleasure.

Gwen is a devoted mother of two sons, and a jubilant grandmother to grandaughter Haylee, who was the inspiration for Gwen's new book; which is written for and dedicated to all the Golfing Grandmothers in the world.

The book, entitled ''Fore My Golfing Grandmother'' is currently selling in stores everywhere.

Gwen is a gourmet cook and hostess ''extraordinaire'' noted for her party extravaganzas. She is also an accomplished fashion and interior designer.

As you turn the following pages you will discover Gwen's passion for life and beauty, as reflected in the ''Greatest Golf Resorts in the World. Enjoy!

*United
States
Resorts*

The Balsams

DIXVILLE NOTCH,
NEW HAMPSHIRE

T he Balsams is a 15,000-acre private pleasure resort in New England where you will be entertained like royalty. Luxurious comfort in a gracious atmosphere of traditional charm will assure you that this will be the experience of a lifetime.

This resort debuted in the late 1800's with the opening of the Dixville House. The Balsams Inn opened in 1873, and in 1917 the new wing, called Hampshire House, was built. The respected legacy of the Balsams is guarded by the New Englanders who are committed to classic hospitality.

The resort itself is picturesquely situated in the natural splendor of sheer mountain walls and a forest wilderness. It can honestly claim the cleanest and healthiest environment in the United States, east of the Rockies. Light-hearted leisure activities make the perfect holiday a reality, not a dream.

 An 18-hole, 6,500-yard championship course designed by famed architect Donald Ross provides you with a panoramic view that extends over two states and Canada. A nine-hole executive course also is available, if you want to improve your short game. Oh, and have I got great news for you: You may play limitless golf, and all for free.

Opportunities in other sports include tennis (with a particularly fashionable tennis shop, all-weather courts, and complimentary clinics), swimming in an Olympic-sized pool, canoeing, badminton, horseshoes, shuffleboard, mountain climbing, or just plain nature walks.

More than 230 guest rooms have been decorated to reflect the grace and charm of the period, but with today's conveniences.

Entertainment varies, but you can count on the Balsams' orchestra to play nightly for your dancing pleasure. During the week, the elegant Switzerland of America Ballroom features star performers, variety acts, comedians, and concert musicians. If you happen to be a night person, there is a late-night piano bar. Films are run for the movie buffs, too.

The Balsams, established as New England's premier resort, is called "the Switzerland of America." It competes favorably with other skiing complexes since the local mountain slopes are well developed for winter sport.

The Balsams is expensive, but you can count on value received. It generally doesn't attract the kind of people who like to show off their folding money: only those who want to have a memorable experience in a gracious setting.

Take time to plan your trip to one of the three Four Star resorts in the Northeast. You'll be glad you did.

"The Switzerland of America"

A golfer's dream for smoothing out your game all at one place: the nine-hole executive Par 32 course for short irons and putting; and the 18-hole championship course to test your long irons, woods and skill.

Concord
Resort
Hotel

KAIMESHA LAKE, NEW YORK

T he Concord at Kaimesha Lake, New York, a multi-million dollar oasis for soaring spirits, has gained a reputation as a "total resort."

Ranked among America's 20 best golf courses, The Concord features two championship layouts.

The International Course of 7,100 yards was completed during post-war days. It is one of the most beautiful and challenging courses you will ever play.

Well aware that a championship course needed champions to show it off, The Concord pursued the services of Dr. Cary Middlecoff, Jackie Burke, Jr., Doug Ford, and Jimmy Demaret who, after the course was built, represented the hotel in the touring pro circuit. I am told that the real stir came when, in one season, The Concord's pros accounted for victories in the Master's, P.G.A. Championships, and the United States Open. Many of the pros still favor these beautiful holes of golf since the course is as plush as Turkish rugs.

"The Monster" is an 18-hole sister course. Each has its own beautiful clubhouse. Last but not least, the Challenger is a nine-hole course that could be just your ticket to sharpen up your short game.

The three courses were designed by famed architect Joe Finger of Houston who says there are three important things a course needs to offer the golfer: 1. It must be pleasing to the eye; 2. It must be enjoyable; 3. It must be a fair test of golf.

We felt he accomplished it all with these courses.

The Concord's 11-story Towers East was recently completed with 200 new rooms, making a total of 1,200 rooms. This is a large complex, to say the least, but we found so many recreational options that it never seemed crowded. All guest quarters are warmly decorated to give you the assurance that, at The Concord, you are a *guest*.

In addition to the main facility, a 40-room clubhouse directly on the new Concord Course offers luxury accommodations for the very avid golfer.

Dining is always a special event at The Concord, featuring American and Old World cuisine. The sumptuous food, served in *grande* surroundings, is always a hit. In the Imperial Room, every seat has an unobstructed view, where you will often find yourself dining with show business personalities and other famous guests staying at the resort.

Can you imagine feeding 3,500 people at one time at one seating? They do it, and I must say they do it well. Using the American Plan, all meals, entertainment, and facilities are covered in one charge rate.

To wind down at the end of the long day, you can have a quiet nightcap or a dance in the Night Owl Lounge.

*"An oasis
for soaring
spirits"*

If you are interested in fitness, there is a $1-million health club with indoor and outdoor skating rinks, swimming pools, and even a skeet-shooting range. Boating, bike riding, archery, handball courts, and great tennis facilities can be enjoyed by the most demanding traveler.

Grossinger's

GROSSINGER, NEW YORK

What began as a tiny boarding house now has expanded to one of the nation's finest resorts. New Yorkers and people from around the world have been visiting Grossinger's since 1914. Privately owned by the Grossinger family, the resort continues to plan, prepare, and please with just the right ingredients for their visitors. Everything here is done on a big scale, making Grossinger's truly a world renowned pleasure resort.

Guest accommodations consist of 600 rooms and suites in the main complex or at Grossinger Lodge, or the Grossinger Hotel & Country Club.

Dining in the elegant main dining room is an exquisite affair and the fun never stops at the Pink Elephant Lounge. In the Terrace Room new and exciting shows are presented nightly and there is no cover or minimum charge.

As a youngster, I vividly remember learning that many show business personalities got their magical break from performing here.

For daytime playing, the Lake and Valley Golf Course has been designed by Joe Finger. The yardage is 6,758 for men, and it is a Par 71.

The course is well known for its fabulous fourth hole (a Par 5 island hole) where the green seems to wind right into the waters of Grossinger's Lake. It's not particularly easy!

Everywhere you look you can see beauty, in the old trees, luscious fairways, and dwarf waterfalls highlighting lovely brooks that meander, crisscrossing the course.

The Vista Nine yardage is 3,288 for men, a Par 36. The course was redesigned by Joe Finger in 1970.

Every attention to detail has been paid to their full facility clubhouse, dining room, locker rooms, and bar, and you will love the golf here at Grossinger's.

Besides health clubs, saunas, and shopping arcade, you can try your skill at swimming indoor and outdoor pools, horseback riding, handball, boating and fishing, and tennis.

For an exciting golf vacation, this is a super recommendation.

*"Everything
on a big scale,
and everywhere
beauty"*

Grossinger's
HOTEL and COUNTRY CLUB

Vacationing in chocolate town can be a sweet golfing experience. Complex above is known as the golf capital of Pennsylvania.

Hershey's "Chocolate Town, U.S.A." has been a sweet spot for golfers for a long time and once you try it, it will be a sweet spot for you, too. You may bed down in one of the spacious rooms in the hotel complex and feel right at home, or you may select an ideal vacation chalet, nestled beautifully in the forest of German pines adjacent to the hotel. Furnished luxuriously, these have been newly renovated and they are ideally located if you like to be close to the big hotel but enjoy the privacy of a quiet forest.

Hershey Lodge features three restaurants and a nightclub, plus its own cinema. Food and service have always been a trademark, helping Hershey attract repeat guests year after year.

Hershey is known as the "Golf Capital of Pennsylvania" and rightly so as they boast three 18-hole golf courses.

The historic Old West Course, built in the 1930's, is now the home of the L.P.G.A. Keystone Open, rated as one of their top tournaments. Old West is ranked as one of America's top 25 country club courses and it continues to be listed among *Golf Digest's* 100 courses. Hole #5 on the West Course was once the front lawn of the home of Milton Hershey, originator of this most unusual resort. Now Mr. Hershey's former home is corporate headquarters for the Hershey Food Company and an important regional landmark.

Hotel Hershey & Country Club

HERSHEY, PENNSYLVANIA

"Great golf, luxury, a theme park, a pine forest, and sweet history"

The new and challenging East Course has three man-made lakes and 100 traps, gorgeous trees, fresh air, and blue skies. Within a mile is one of America's top public courses, Hershey Parkview Golf; Hotel Hershey's own nine-hole course, carved in a sea of German pines; and nine-hole, Spring Creek Golf, just east of town.

There's never a dull moment for the vacationing golfer in this chocolate town, where you may visit the ever-popular theme park. Chocolate kisses for street lamps adorn the streets, and the entertainment is continuous. Dolphin and sea lion shows, country and western musical performances are only a part of what's in store for guests.

Visiting the factory to see the processes used in making Hershey's delicious candy bars is an experience you won't forget. And a leisurely stroll through their award-winning gardens can add a pretty touch to your day. There are 23 acres of continuous flower displays, and in April and May over 45,000 tulips are in bloom.

The hotel complex is recognized for tennis and for many other outdoor sports, and it could be a perfect spot for a convention. Next time you get a sweet tooth for a chocolate-coated golfing experience, head for the Hotel Hershey and Country Club. They'll be waiting.

Traveling golfers can enjoy continuous fun at the theme park, above.

The Mount Washington

BRETTON WOODS, NEW HAMPSHIRE

*"Grandeur
plus
graciousness
equals
serenity"*

Discovering the charm of Mount Washington was a charm indeed. The stately white towers of the Edwardian masterpiece are surrounded by the grandeur of Mount Washington and the Presidential Range, evoking a feeling of the graciousness of bygone days.

The Mount Washington, grandest of all resorts in the White Mountains, was built by Joseph Stickney, who made a fortune in coal and the Pennsylvania Railroad. For over 80 years, this resort has been steeped in a tradition of friendly and attentive service. Catering throughout the years to very wealthy and fashionable guests has been a training ground for pleasing the particular.

Whatever your individual need in accommodations, they have it. If you prefer one of the newly renovated rooms, you may choose from Family, Tourister, Standard, Luxor and Parlor. If you are a bit on the contemporary side, they can serve you in the Lodge at Bretton Woods, with indoor and outdoor swimming pools. Townhouses, too, are popular here with every modern convenience.

Not only will you see the stars at night, but you will have your own stars performing for you as you dine. "The Brettonians," talented singers, make your meal an entertainment treat as well as a culinary delight. And I promise you, your food will be as exquisite as your service and the atmosphere. The pleasant Ammonoosuc Dining Room features their own orchestra to put you in the mood for a great evening. Serving elegant continental fare, they certainly gained my applause.

Stickney's Restaurant, located in the lower lobby of the hotel, is open for tasty lunches and special events, with its own intimate lounge. Darby's Tavern is the perfect spot for more divine food in a warm, rustic setting. The Princess Lounge, located off the hotel lobby, always has live music and attracts a crowd.

Recreational facilites are numerous, but of course, golf on this P.G.A. course, designed by Donald Ross, is a tradition.

The links have been graced with many a famous golfer, including Babe Ruth and Bobby Jones. Now this course is the home of a new golf academy run by a working associate of Ken

Venturi. It's a place where many professionals come to retreat and for coaching. Why not you?

As you wind among the great evergreens and rushing trout streams, you will touch base with Mother Nature in a big way. A typical hill and dale course, it is challenging and relentlessly scenic, winding through forests and glades, crossing the Ammonoosuc River twice, and full of eye-filling mountain views.

The #14 hole is rated as one of the best Par 3's in New England. A Par 71, the course measures 6,154 yards from the whites.

The newly restored nine-hole course, which is located to the front of the hotel, now enables you to sharpen up your short game, too.

Tennis, indoor and outdoor swimming, as well as horseback riding, hiking, and dancing, offer a welcome change of pace.

If you want to find serenity and escape to improve or enjoy your game, you can give #1 priority to The Mount Washington. It's well worth it.

C ape Cod needs no formal introduction as we have all heard
about this wonderful place even through song, but introduc-
ing this large recreational resort is a pleasure. Extending over
2,700 acres, it is one of the most ambitious planned resorts in the
Northeast. Every effort was made to insure harmonious association

with the environment and to make this a choice seaside creation.

Accommodations are at the New Seabury Inn, which is sited on a bluff overlooking Nantucket Sound, or at cottages nestled along the oceanfront at the Popponesset Inn, one of Cape Cod's oldest and best known seaside inns.

Beautifully decorated interiors, resembling a private home, are complemented by balconies or sun decks and in most units there are full kitchens or kitchenettes.

Accommodations at the Popponesset Inn, which is open from June to mid-September, are located on a rise overlooking the ocean. Most have fireplaces and some have kitchens, and they are so comfortable that many of their guests call Popponesset their "summer home" and return repeatedly.

Commanding one of the Cape's most beautiful views of Nantucket Sound and Martha's Vineyard, the New Seabury Inn Restaurant and Lounge offers superb cuisine prepared and served with a Continental accent. You can relax and enjoy a drink while taking in the drama of the glorious sunsets.

Popponesset Inn at the water's edge has always been one of the Cape's favorite restaurants. You can dine outside on the deck and watch the moon rise over the shimmering ocean. Entertainment and dancing are enjoyed by all.

Bobby Byrne's Pub is a delightful change of pace with warm and friendly atmosphere typical of an English pub. It is opened all year.

On The Rocks Lounge is one of the Cape's top night spots — a perfect place to listen, dance, or just enjoy.

New Seabury

ON CAPE COD, MASSACHUSETTS

Due to the proximity to the Gulf Stream, New Seabury is a year-round golf resort. As a guest at either hotel, you will have full country club privileges and here you can choose from two 18-hole golf courses.

The Blue Championship Course is a Par 72 and is 7,175 yards long; the Green Challenger Course is a Par 70.

The Blue Course is listed by *Golf Digest* as one of America's 100 most testing courses. Sparkling ponds, salt marshes, and pines are highlighted by the well-groomed fairways and manicured greens. It is the home of many major New England tournaments.

Waterside fairways with on-shore breezes can demand a premium of your accuracy. The hills and valleys, however, make it more substantially sheltered from the Cape's whimsical winds.

The Blue Course is closed to all but club members, but as a guest at New Seabury or Popponesset you may play as much golf as you desire.

"Year-round golfing on Cape Cod"

Tennis is here in a big way with 16 all-weather courts. Horseback riding and swimming, plus beaching on their five miles of salt water beach, are great. Sailing, fishing, bicycling, and walking through flora and fauna can only add perfectly to your day.

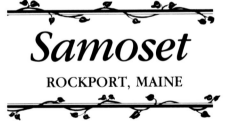

Samoset

ROCKPORT, MAINE

This is truly a luxurious year-round resort overlooking Penob-scot Bay on the mid-Maine coast. You will long remember the spectacular vistas of the rugged coast, the Bay, and off-shore islands. Host in the past to many famous personalities, the Samoset has a unique ambience in the true spirit of the "grand hotel" of yesteryear.

One hundred and fifty new rooms, all with their own private balconies overlooking the Bay, offer their guests tasteful decor. You may choose from one or two-bedroom suites, with large private patios.

Dining at Samoset is a "happening" in the true sense of the word. You may dine on Continental delicacies or a hearty New England repast.

In the Bay Point Dining Room you will find fresh lobster like none other, as well as prime beef dinners. Cocktails may be sipped in the intimate lounge where floor-to-ceiling windows allow you breathtaking views of the gracious grounds and of the Bay. Tip top entertainment is a guarantee that your night will be hoppin'!

While enjoying all of this, you can't help but be mesmerized, sitting and looking out at the boats, vistas of lighthouses, ships, and schooners, as well as the off-shore islands and the glittering Atlantic Ocean. Just beyond the rolling greens of the golf course, the Break-waters run straight into the Bay for almost a mile where it is crowned by Rockland Light, a symbol of safety for the local men at sea.

Speaking of golf, Samoset's championship 6,285-yard layout from the blue tees; features eight ocean-front holes making this one of the loveliest courses in New England.

The views are as demanding as the course, but I can tell you the exhilaration you will feel as you play among these lush green rolling fairways, surrounded totally by trees, water, and the unspoiled environment will make you happy you chose Samoset.

"Something for everyone"

Tennis, swimming, saunas, and exercise rooms are a few of the other enticements. If you are planning a meeting and need lovely conference facilities they have these, too.

For the adventurous and the romantic, a cruise leaves nightly with fine champagne, fun, and good company. They say "you haven't fully appreciated Maine until you have viewed her from the water."

Sugarloaf/USA

KINGSFIELD, MAINE

Beautiful countryside, unspoiled air, fabulous golf and varied sporting options.

Sugarloaf/USA is a very unique area with mixes and blends of architecture, restaurants and fun-filled sports. Surrounded by the Western mountains of Maine, you will discover an exciting personality here.

Your accommodations are offered in a variety of choices. Right on the mountain on the ski slope or on the golf course, you can select a hotel room, studio apartment, or a five bedroom condominium. Sugarloaf Inn has many rentals to choose from also. All decorated and comfortable befitting the all around atmosphere.

For dining the newest addition for elegant dining is the "Narrow Gauge Station," featuring wonderful cuisine and some of the most spectacular views of Maine.

The Seasons at Sugarloaf Inn include the Greenhouse dining room with an elegant touch. For your favorite cocktails don't miss the Widowmaker Lounge at the new "Base Lodge."

If you are a horseman, there are over 900 square miles of wilderness, woods, cross country runs and nature trails. You will thrill if you are a hiker, while hiking on the Mountain, the second highest in Maine.

 Robert Trent Jones, Jr's business is constructing famous golf courses in favored places.

This golf course is one of the few courses built in a wilderness, which was at one time dense, viewless, and almost non-traversible.

This new 18-hole Sugarloaf Golf Club course will offer players some of the most spectacular scenery in the United States.

It is a breathtakingly beautiful course, very bold, yet won't overwhelm the beginner.

The woods play an integral part since it is 90% wooded.

Measuring 6,898 yards from the championship tees it is a Par 72.

Tennis, fishing, boating plus a health and fitness spa are yours to enjoy, plus the gondola rides up the mountain can be fabulous fun "weather permitting." Famous to the surrounding area are the white water rapids.

Don't forget to stroll through the Alpine Village and see the quaint shops. Also surrounding this area are historical little towns. You will love seeing Maine take on a new personality.

Woodstock Inn & Resort

WOODSTOCK, VERMONT

"Everything that a quaint town of Yankeedom should possess"

This three-story, 86-year-old Inn exemplifies the spirit of colonialism in its understated atmosphere. The setting is a Vermont village; the Inn itself is on the Village Green. In 1969, Laurance Rockefeller replaced the Inn, but the tradition of the earlier Inns was maintained. Now a member of the Rockresorts, it has been refurbished in the typical manner, keeping with New England tradition.

Each of the 120 rooms is adorned with a homemade patchwork quilt, offering a friendly and warm stay. Surrounded by all the beautiful landscaped gardens and native trees, you will love your visit to New England.

Being Vermont's first golf course makes this a very "UNIQUE COURSE." It was laid out in 1895 in a cow pasture on Mt. Peg in Woodstock. Famed golf architect Robert Trent Jones says it is one of the most interesting short club courses in the nation. He should know; he re-designed it in 1963.

The course is nestled in the Kedron Valley and is geographically challenging and picturesque as it winds its way on the valley floor, among rolling hills. Blending perfectly with the surroundings, it is literally sculpted into the natural contours of the valley. Though it is a relatively short course — Par 69, 6,043 yards for championship play — it demands accuracy. Water comes into play 11 times, and that's a lot of water to deal with. The best time to plan a visit for golf would be from May through foliage time. The weather and scenery cannot be beat.

The temperature at Woodstock rarely goes above 90 degrees during the summers, and nights are "guaranteed cool." The climate is dry, but oh so healthy. This is one of the few spots left where you and *"Mother Nature"* can truly get reacquainted.

The history of Woodstock is unusual and colorful. Renowned for preserving both the physical setting and the spiritual flavor of an earlier day, "much of the village" has been designated an Historic District. You will enjoy all the quaint and authentic homes, covered bridges, and of course the Paul Revere Bells will be music to your ears. Woodstock is one of the prettiest towns according to *National Geographic,* and you will probably agree, too.

The Inn is known for its hot and hearty New England fare, part of which is made up of local plants such as Vermont's fiddlehead ferns and morel mushrooms. Among the guests' most popular entrees, interestingly enough, is seafood. Being an award-winning restaurant, they offer a lot of tips, recipes, and photo opportunities the year round for their guests.

Besides the main dining room, your other options consist of a coffee shop and The Pine Room for cocktails and entertainment. At the Country Club is another dining room and bar for refreshments before or after golf. Tennis is available as is swimming, mountain exploring, and of course shopping in this most historical, charming village.

If you enjoy picking up on a little history and turning back the pages of time to see how your ancestors may have lived, you are in for a real treat.

The Woodstock Inn is easily accessible from all major cities by train, car, or by bus.

Amelia Island

**AMELIA ISLAND PLANTATION,
FLORIDA**

When we arrived here by car at this gloriously peaceful and private resort, the loudest thing we heard was the crashing of the surf or the clip-clop of a horse and rider. Amelia Island is at the southernmost end of the large Atlantic Golden Isles. It is a symphony of massive sand dunes, golden sea coasts, and hideaway lagoons flowing into tidal marshlands. It was so peaceful that we hated to leave because we felt we were in a world of our own.

The resort feels as though it was removed from the mainstream of time, yet it is only 29 miles from Jacksonville International Airport.

The setting is still fresh in my mind as I remember one particular hole of the course between us and the splashing ocean. Speaking of the golf course, 27 challenging holes, designed by Pete Dye, will live in your memory long after your visit has ended. Oakmarsh and Oysterbay nines have winding fairways, marsh edges, and undulating greens. Oceanside, the third nine, includes three holes nestled between sand dunes and paralleling the sea. These are sporty courses and extremely interesting; each hole has its own character, but your work is cut out for you because as beautiful as they are, they are equally as challenging. The rough will test your concentration, and as a matter of fact, can be downright frustrating.

Truly spacious and dramatically designed are the one, two, three, and four-bedroom villas with every appointment carefully chosen. Some of the private villas overlook the golf course and the ocean beyond — a spectacular "happening" to say the least. We will never forget it. Besides being a favorite of ours, everyone who has been here shares our enthusiasm.

At the remarkably sophisticated and charming Duneside Club, continental cuisine is served in a romantic setting overlooking the ocean. The Amelia Island Inn, with its 125-seat oceanview restaurant and cocktail lounge, is the social head of the plantation. The Veranda Restaurant serves the tastiest seafoods and the Admiral's Lounge features fine live entertainment to accompany refreshing drinks and relaxing conversation.

This resort is rated as one of the Top 10 Resorts by *Florida Trend* magazine. I feel that it is an honor to rate it as excellent and on top of our list, too.

Aside from the great golf, the plantation is the home of the Women's Tennis Association Championships. It has been rated as one of America's top 50 by *Tennis Magazine,* and is the home of Chris Evert and John Lloyd.

Additional sports include swimming, biking, and fishing.

Amelia is still as naturally beautiful as it was when it was named for the lovely daughter of King George more than 200 years ago.

"Removed from the mainstream of time"

Boca Raton Hotel and Club

BOCA RATON, FLORIDA

A combination of lavish grounds, service, cuisine, and accommodations brings golfers back again and again.

The Boca Raton Hotel and Club is one of the most beautiful and celebrated golfing resorts in the world. Created in 1926 to cater to the exacting tastes of millionaires, crowned heads, and film stars, it is a tropical paradise. The Five-Star resort, now managed by the Arvida Corporation, offers unexcelled food, accommodations, service, and a surprisingly challenging golf course.

The resort's reputation for serving superior cuisine in an elegant setting is justly deserved no matter which dining room a guest selects. In each, master chefs prepare every entree to order, taking no shortcuts and using only the finest fresh ingredients.

The guest has several dining rooms to select from, each offering its special ambience. The Patio and Cathedral Dining Room is a favorite of many in the evenings for dinner and dancing featuring the upbeat music of a society band. Top of the Towers is another favorite for its glorious view. The beach club's Cabana Dining Room is popular, and so is the Shell, a reservations-only, split-level continental dining room. And golfers, seeking a mid-day respite, find the food at the Four Lions to their liking.

The accommodations at the resort are as lavish as the grounds and cuisine. Guests can stay in the main hotel, in villas, in the tower, or at the beach club. Each offers a bit of a different experience.

In the courtyard, the legendary "Lady" gives a warm welcome to guests as they enter the main gate.

This is a resort which pampers its guests. There is one employee per guest to respond to any need.

But, of course, we visit Boca Raton to play golf. The course here is challenging for the skilled golfer but because of its unusual beauty, an amateur enjoys it as much. It has been home to Tommy Armour and Sam Snead, both of whom have served as host professionals. The 18-hole championship course challenges you with doglegs, large traps, and huge rubber trees.

Even if the Boca Raton course weren't so challenging, it would attract you because of its manicured fairways, tropical gardens, colorful flowers, and excitement. Each hole has its own beauty. But the favorite of many is the 18th, which is framed by the dramatic hotel and tower.

As if the glorious hotel course were not enough, as their guest you have an opportunity to play equally interesting courses at the 72-hole nearby Boca West Resort.

Boca Raton is a year-round resort, with temperatures averaging in the 70's in winter and 80's in summer. Thus sportswear and informal dress are appropriate by day, more formal dress including coats and ties for gentlemen in the evening.

"Its reputation for superior cuisine is justly deserved"

The Breakers

PALM BEACH, FLORIDA

A place you will never forget, The Breakers is a truly elegant and magnificent hotel. It has earned both Mobil's Five Star Award and the AAA Five Diamond Award. The Breakers was built by Henry Morrison Flager, and his heirs maintain the hotel in keeping with the Flager tradition. It is a perfect blend of old world majesty and new world convenience. The charm here lies in the hotel's heritage.

This is one of the "grande hotels" with vaulted ceilings and innumerable antiques and art objects. Your eyes have an immediate feast. If sophisticated vacationing is your style, you will relate to this magnificent hotel.

A perfect blend of Old World majesty and New World convenience.

Starting with your first game, you'll feel great about your choice of golf courses. The Ocean Course, an 18-hole course designed by Donald Ross, is lined with beautiful Florida palms. It was built at the turn of the century. Though it is a Par 70 and 6,008 yards, this course demands attention and strategy.

The West Course, designed by Willard Byrd, is situated on 460 acres and is approximately a 20-minute drive from the hotel proper. It is a championship course with a rating of 73.7, Par 71, and 7,101 yards.

Both courses have their own beautiful pro shops and dining rooms. The Ocean Course also has its own health department, complete with sauna and masseur.

Tennis, biking, jogging, and aquatic sports are optional recreational opportunities.

Nighttime is a dream at The Breakers, and that is why my husband and I frequent this glorious place. It is not difficult to relive the romance of the Old World amid the old charm. Candidly speaking, as much as I loved my golf, I would have to say that my mind kept wandering, thinking about the romantic evening we were about to enjoy. If you want your days to end gloriously, and if you are a bit of a romanticist, you can anticipate an evening of festivities not to be forgotten. We slipped into an intimate mood as we embraced the ambience created by the elegant decor, the music, savoring our cocktails, and enjoying the finest in dining, dancing and cuisine.

The Breakers is located on the island of Palm Beach, Florida, 65 miles north of Miami and four miles from Palm Beach International Airport. One nice touch for the international traveler: the staff of more than 1,200 speaks a total of 28 foreign languages.

"A must for the international traveler"

"Everything is satisfactual"

Broadwater Beach Hotel

BILOXI, MISSISSIPPI

The theme of the Broadwater Beach is "Everything is Satisfactual," and they certainly live up to it! As one of America's great incentive resorts, the Broadwater Beach offers a happy combination of old-fashioned Southern hospitality, surroundings of natural beauty, and first class resort amenities.

Their 33 acres of beautifully landscaped flowering gardens, emerald lawns, and spreading oak trees tantalize the eye and soothe the spirit. A total of 360 rooms and suites provide plenty of luxurious choices, but if you prefer, they have villas, too — totally deluxe and very tastefully done.

"FOOD" is a Southern tradition, and you'll find no exception here with four great restaurants to select from. If you're looking for a regal evening, try the Royal Terrace, where the cuisine is on stage and always a "star." The Patio will add to your casual pleasures, or try the Lanai Lounge adjacent to the pool. Nautical and informal, they specialize in seafood, always fresh and guaranteed to hit the spot.

Entertainment always draws a crowd, and you probably will be no exception. For your dancing enjoyment, an orchestra plays nightly.

Golf on the Gulf is always fun. If you choose the thickly wooded but thin fairways of the Sea Course, you will have some terrific views of the Gulf, along with chances of putting your ball there, too. Tall pines and spreading oaks can pester you and your drives, and you may not forgive the devilish traps. But do we ever???

The Sun Course, newest and toughest, has a lot of water, palms, pines, and flower beds to admire. But keep your eye on the ball. Duffers find this course playable, while touring pros find it challenging. The truth is that most everyone finds it fair, and that is really what counts. Try it and find out.

Not to be overlooked is the Fun Course. Even the pros use this to smooth out their irons. It is night-lighted in case you don't get enough golf during the day.

Day or night tennis is another option, along with croquet, ping pong, volleyball, and badminton. The three-tiered Lanai Pool is one of two heated swimming pools, and 26 miles of white, sandy beaches along the Gulf offer more aquatic opportunities, while helping to make this resort one of the finest in the region.

Republic Airlines services Biloxi Gulfport from all over the country, so for authentic Southern hospitality and tradition, the Broadwater Beach is a convenient and truly memorable choice.

allaway Gardens is known today as one of the choicest golf resorts in Georgia. Being among its 2,500 acres of garden beauty is the thrill of a lifetime. As we drove on the property, I was literally stunned by the beauty surrounding us. It was springtime and all the flowering crabapple trees, azaleas, and magnolias were in full bloom. However, we were told companion flowers offer year-round beauty. Be sure to take the scenic drive. I cannot expound enough on it.

The most refreshing thing we found at Callaway was their dedication to beauty and the pride they take in it.

Accommodations vary a great deal, providing a different option for everyone. The rustic cottages are comfortable, but certainly not fancy. The Inn rooms are typical hotel rooms and are located near the conference centers and restaurants. The Mountain Creek Villas give you a choice of one to four bedrooms. All have private patios as well as fireplaces and kitchens and are furnished in early American or contemporary.

 The other beauty at Callaway is the 63 holes of golf you have to choose from. The Mountain View course was designed by world-famous Joe Lee. It is a Par 72 and is 18 holes and 7,040 yards of wonderful but rugged challenge. They say, "If you can beat Mountain View, you can beat just about any course."

Lakeview is very scenic and interesting, a Par 70, with wide fairways that wind across Mountain Creek Lake. The famous island tee adds an element of drama to your game.

The Garden View Course is the newest 18-hole layout and has bent grass greens. It presents a little more fun and is particularly beautiful, as its name implies.

The Garden View Course is rated 69.7 from the back tees against a Par of 72. It is a good test of golf for your shotmaking ability and can prove helpful for your game management.

Last, but certainly not least, is the sweet little nine-hole executive, the Sky View. A well-groomed and very challenging little number, it measures 2,096 yards.

After fun playing golf most of the day, much more awaits you in the evening with an array of restaurants to choose from — the Plantation Room for lavish Southern cooking, the Georgia Room serving Continental cuisine in a traditional manner (we found this to be a real winner), or Country Kitchen for any meal served in country style. For your more quiet and intimate needs, a Lounge offers nightly entertainment and is enjoyed by all.

Biking, hiking, walking, and horseback riding are popular sports at Callaway, as is skeet and trap shooting. They have their own lovely beach, a haven for sun-worshippers. But though there is a sport for anyone here, GOLF is the premier activity.

After you have visited Callaway Gardens, they want you to take home "consolation for the heart, nourishment for the soul, and inspiration for the mind."

Callaway Gardens

PINE MOUNTAIN, GEORGIA

The ever-popular buffet serves Southern cooking at its finest.

"Consolation for the heart, nourishment for the soul, inspiration for the mind"

The Cloister

SEA ISLAND, GEORGIA

Above, The Cloister's gracious Spanish Lounge, a favorite of all guests.

One of the most outstanding seaside Retreat Plantations provides a unique setting for The Cloister. The plantation, in its great antebellum days, was famous for the quality of its Sea Island cotton. Now it is distinctive worldwide for this grand hotel and grand golf.

The famed golf courses have attracted many professionals, including Walter Travis, Bobby Jones, Sam Snead, Mickey Wright, and Louise Suggs. Travis helped design the original nine, which opened in 1928. (There are four nines here, each individually designed.) Jones and Snead were longtime course record holders. Tony Jacklin played out of Sea Island when he won his triple crown, and Mickey Wright calls this her favorite course. Louise Suggs conducts her highly regarded golf clinics here in which you can participate. As a guest you may also play the 18 holes at the Island Club.

Seaside #7 is often people's favorite because it is the most difficult for pros, but attainable for all others. The Sea Island courses are played the year around, and the pro shop is one of the more attractive and better stocked shops anywhere. Whether you need golf attire or some special sports clothes, you will find it a pleasure to shop here. (The Cloister's main building also offers a variety of excellent shops.)

When you think of the world's great resort hotels, the Cloister always comes to mind. Even overseas honors have been won, the newest from the *World Hotel Guide,* its Crown Award which is the *Guide's* code for the very best.

A host of new honors have been given the Cloister, including the Mobil Five-Star and the Five Diamond AAA Award. It was voted one of the world's greatest hotels by World Traveler Touring Club, and *Town and Country* says it is one of "1983's greatest getaways."

Each guest enjoys a choice of different low-rise accommodations scattered around the main Cloister building, either on the beach or nearby. They are tastefully decorated and delightful with the ring of the "early South." Period furnishings have been incorporated in the main part of the hotel, too, which is always a joy to visit because of the art objects, antiques, and splendid views opening onto the colorful courtyard replete with waterfalls.

Meals are included in your fare, and the service is exquisite. The prestigious Ivy Award, bestowed by *Restaurant and Institution Magazine,* has been given recently for excellence in food. Dining is also available at the golf course. The exclusive clientele ensures an extra bonus of interesting people to see and meet.

A host of other sports facilities includes skeet, tennis, and riding. The five-mile stretch of private beach makes this resort complete, and is enjoyed by all.

Sea Island

"Distinctive worldwide for its grand hotel"

Left, the Avenue of the Oaks reminds golfers of the antebellum plantation past of this unique resort. Below, the South Patio.

One of America's most sumptuous hotels, Williamsburg Inn's pre-eminence has been documented over the decades by numerous honors and recognition, including the Mobil Travel Guide's highest five-star rating.

My husband agreed with me on our last visit that the Inn's secret is the great effort they make to provide luxury with no fuss. It's a popular spot for celebrated people as well as busy people, and marvelous if you just want to "run away from it all" and relax.

As an Inn, the ambience and mystique touched a tender spot in my heart. And as a resort, of course, we thoroughly loved both golf courses.

Colonial Williamsburg Inn

WILLIAMSBURG, VIRGINIA

The Golden Horseshoe utilizes all of Mother Nature's idiosyncrasies and, believe me, she was generous here. Spreading over 125 acres of rolling terrain, its fairways stretch around a five-acre lake, up ravines, and down dense woodland valleys. Another championship 18-hole course, magnificently designed by Rees Jones, has captivated the heart of many golf lovers.

The name Golden Horseshoe originated with Williamsburg's Governor Alexander Spotswood, who led his daring expedition from Williamsburg over the Appalachian Mountains. Upon returning, Spotswood honored each expedition member with a golden horseshoe.

Complementing this 18-holer is the adjoining nine-hole Spotswood course, complete with lakes, wooded glens, and cushioned turf. Great fun prevails on these tricky, dog-legged fairways.

"Luxury with no fuss"

The Inn has 166 rooms and has played to a wide audience, including many U.S. presidents, Queen Elizabeth, and numerous royalty from other countries.

When Mr. and Mrs. John D. Rockefeller, Jr., made plans for the Inn, they wanted it to have the feeling of a home-away-from-home, rather than expressing a hotel atmosphere. This philosophy dictates today's style and furnishings, along with the service. Dining, for example, is perfect, with candlelight, flowers, and glittering silver. The dignity and elegance in the Regency Room is unimaginable. Sitting in such splendor, plus enjoying other more casual moments, made our stay memorable.

Blending the old with the new, Williamsburg features an historic "time walk" that reminds us of the wonderful tasks our forefathers performed. As you walk away from these tours, it adds a dimension to your life as an American.

The Diplomat

HOLLYWOOD, FLORIDA

Truly superior quality never happens by accident. At the Diplomat, the staff makes sure superior quality is constant. We found the staff to be exceptionally well-trained, which touched our souls.

Situated in a sub-tropical setting in the city of Hollywood, Florida, the hotel is located south of the Hollywood-Ft. Lauderdale airport and 15 miles from Miami Beach. A unique feature is that the hotel is a family-owned and operated business.

The facilities feature the Diplomat East and the luxurious Tower Building on the oceanside. They are inviting to say the least. The Diplomat West extends comfortably along the waterway and encourages informality. The 600 acres of resort area is in a lush tropical setting, with 1,200 handsomely decorated rooms, suites, and penthouse suites. Each room has its own Home Box Office movies 24 hours a day.

To appease any appetite, there are nine restaurants to choose from, if you want French cuisine, steaks, seafood, or just plain coffeeshop fare. There are two country club dining rooms as well as an intimate Inn. And more . . .

Three lounges offer entertainment and dancing nightly. The Tack Room has continuous bands and dancing for your pleasure. The Celebrity Room attracts patrons from all over the country with the staff's lavish attention to every detail in service and cuisine.

The Diplomat has the prestige of being rated one of the Top 10 resorts in the world in 1979, 1980, and 1981. It is famous for attracting world-renowned personalities, including U.S. presidents, designers, sports figures, and celebrities.

The thing I enjoyed most was the way they made everyone feel like a celebrity, too.

Among its other awards, the Diplomat is one of the Gold Key Award winners for outstanding food, service, and sports facilities.

There is never a problem scheduling a golf game as they have two championship courses amid rolling greens and tropical trees. The Presidential Country Club course is the championship course laid out for a golfer of any calibre. If you seek beauty in your golf course, you will find it here, along with the aura of tranquility in the abundant flowers, trees, and water. But watch out for the many traps. You can get out of them eventually; ask me, I know. (By the way, it's not uncommon to be teeing off behind someone famous.)

The Diplomat Country Club course also requires accuracy; it's a sporty course with a lot of wonderful distractions. Just keep your eye on the ball. It is a course that is a favorite among celebrities and locals alike.

While the club is known for its fabulous Racquet Club, there are also five swimming pools, a major marina for pleasure fishing and water sports, two health spas for women and men, and a chiropractor on the premises.

We found many exciting and important happenings during our visit, and you can't help but do the same in the city where the sun always shines.

I want to pay special tribute to Irving and Marge Cowan, who have created this giant for all of us to enjoy. It truly represents a dream that became a reality.

"They make everyone feel like a celebrity"

*Eighty-one holes of golf
are just a stroll from
your room*

Doral Hotel and Country Club is situated on 2,400 tropical acres, with 650 guest rooms and suites, plus 32 meeting rooms. If you elect, you may also stay at the Doral Hotel On-the-Ocean, at Miami Beach, which has 420 guest rooms and suites plus 20 meeting rooms, where miles of white beach extend you a real welcome.

The Doral continues to be a haven for celebrities from all walks of life and is an "in" spot for golfers especially. As a truly self-contained resort, Doral offers a diverse selection of restaurants and lounges.

You may wish to begin your day with breakfast at the Gazebo or enjoy a Sandpiper buffet. Hearty sandwiches are served at the Staggerbush Bar, and outdoors on the patio, the Gazebo Coffee Shop has a complete menu. For dinner you may dine *al fresco* amid lush greenery in the Garden Terrace, where you will be served the finest continental specialties available. After dinner, you may want to stop off at the Blue Room Lounge for dancing and a show.

No matter what you choose, you will find fine cuisine and service a hallmark of Doral.

Due to the country club design, Doral's 650 rooms and suites are located in eight separate lodges of various sizes, and they fan out on both sides of the main clubhouse and front directly on the golf courses.

The accommodations are luxurious in the extreme, and most guest rooms boast their own terraces. Bright, exciting color coordinations offer a spark to your already happy environment.

Two other buildings housing 90 guest rooms and suites each are joined in the center with an attractive lobby.

The Doral

MIAMI BEACH, FLORIDA

 As a guest, you may play any of the 81 holes of golf free of charge. Famed as the home of the Doral Eastern Open, the Blue Course will be no stranger to you. But there are three other 18-hole courses and a nine-hole Par 3 also.

The Blue Course is for those who like a challenge. It is 7,065 yards and the pros themselves have dubbed it as the "Monster." It has been rated among the top three most challenging courses on the T.P.A. tour, and IBM computers rate its 18th hole as the toughest Par 4 of them all.

Even with its international reputation, its many lakes, traps everywhere, and tricky greens, the Blue still holds attraction for the average golfer.

The Red Course was designed for pure fun, and is ideal for those who don't enjoy the more strenuous workout. Plush fairways, colorful flowers, and small silky greens invite a light touch.

The White Course is the surprise! Longer than the Red, shorter than the Blue, the 6,659 yards combine some of the features of the other two. Don't get overconfident on the White wonder; it is tricky.

For yardage, the Gold Course is an 18-hole beauty. It is nearly as long as the Blue, 6,863 yards from the championship tees. It has been a controversial course since it was opened as it has been officially rated by both pros and amateurs as a definite challenge to the "Blue Monster."

The Green Course is the nine-hole Par 3 with a glamorous setting, combining trees and the Dolphin Lake. It provides interest as well as fun under the palms and sunshine.

"Luxurious in the extreme"

Numerous other sporting facilities include tennis complexes, swimming, biking, volleyball, basketball, fishing, and men's and women's health clubs.

Famed for luxury and elegance, Doral is an adventure in itself. Facilities and services of the Doral Hotel and Country Club include a convention center, grand ballroom, and numerous other meeting rooms. You may shop at the boutique, with men's and ladies' apparel and a superior pro shop, featuring quality sportswear and newest fashions designed exclusively for Doral.

If you want a memorable golfing experience, this premier resort can go to the top of your list.

Fairfield Glade

FAIRFIELD GLADE, TENNESSEE

Located on the Cumberland Plateau between Knoxville and Nashville, this recreational and resort community consists of 12,371 acres. The 100 room lodge has an indoor swimming pool and sauna plus 20 villas all well-decorated, and comfortable.

Since it is located between the Northern and Southern Appalachian Mountain Range the scenic beauty is unsurpassed.

For casual dining a visit to the Greenhouse Restaurant or the Stonehenge is a satisfying experience. If you elect a more formal evening the Druid Hills Country Club could be a nice choice, as they feature live entertainment, dancing, and a dinner theater.

Attracting the most avid golfer their three 18-hole championship golf courses offer an exciting challenge and a lot of golf.

The newer course "Stonehenge" was designed by Architect Joe Lee. It is one of the most picturesque courses we have played.

Bentgrass tees, fairways and greens have been used, along with magnificent use of the natural settings and terrain. 6,549 yards long it is rated 70 with 63 sand traps. Dorchester is 6,406 yards long with a rating of 70. Bentgrass tees and bluegrass fairways offer a pleasant round among the towering trees. Druid Hills is a private country club, and guests of the Inn may play it, but only with a member. The yardage is 6,329, the rating is 70.4.

Aside from golf the John Newcombe Tennis Center, offers an indoor-outdoor complex with 8 lighted courts for year around play.

There are nine lakes if you care to fish, as well as stables, hiking and a riding trail. The conference center accommodates up to 400 people.

Close by is a 40,000-square foot shopping center for you shop-o-holics....

Swimming and boating add to the endless sporting amenities here.

Fairfield Glade 3 championship courses plus a deluxe 18-hole miniature golf course

Greenbrier

WHITE SULPHUR SPRINGS, WEST VIRGINIA

All the comforts of home in an Eighteenth Century atmosphere.

Mirroring the moods and modes of social America for 205 years, the Greenbrier in White Sulphur Springs is a national historic landmark that derives its splendor from the panoramic elegance of the Allegheny Mountains.

Covering 6,500 acres of unparalleled beauty, the accommodations at the Greenbrier include a range of rooms and spacious parlors, each one different in decor. Privacy and comfort add to your "perfect vacation."

Coming by their Mobil Five Star and Triple A Five Diamond Awards seems quite natural to them, as they have won numerous other national and international awards.

Included in your daily tariff is superb dining offered in one of several dining rooms that express warm and intimate atmospheres. Six course dinners are prepared by a culinary staff of 162, including 35 chefs, and the Tavern Room is a popular spot to enhance an evening.

At the golf club, you may order from the menu or help yourself to their buffet luncheons, all the while enjoying the rolling greens of the golf courses.

The Greenbrier Coffee Shoppe and Ice Cream Parlor is a pleasant alternative for breakfast or lunch—especially if you are not counting calories. For a change of pace, nibble the complimentary hors d'oeuvres served daily in the Old White Club, mixed with a lot of camaraderie.

Three 18-hole championship golf courses should satisfy any golfer's dream. Historically, in 1910, golf was the name of the game and in that year the Greenbrier opened its first course, the 9-hole Lakeside. Four years later, the club added the 18-hole Old White Course; and in 1925 another 18-hole course, the Greenbrier, was built. Lakeside was expanded in 1962, and in 1977 the Greenbrier course (redesigned under the expertise of Jack Nicklaus and lengthened to a par 72) was designated as the site of the Ryder Cup matches. When I think of Greenbrier, I "see" the large yellow awnings billowing over their well-stocked pro shop. All courses begin and end at the pro shop!

Of course, the 12 acres of formal gardens and walkways are also a beautiful memory, and I can't forget our carriage ride and the quaint historical shops and grounds tour. To finish your day on the golf course, the famous Greenbrier Spa is a perfect spot to relax.

For tennis buffs, 15 Hartru outdoor surfaces and five Dynaturf indoor courts await you. Bicycling, horseback riding, jogging, bowling, fishing, and exercising contribute to your athletic pleasures.

There are 1,400 employees to pamper guests 24 hours a day (linens are changed twice daily, for example, and your bed is turned down; a chocolate mint is laid on your pillow). Who could ask for more? The allure of Greenbrier is conducive to the best of all possible golfing vacations.

When you think of Greenbrier, you automatically think of the great Sam Snead.

"An historic landmark and a favorite"

Grenelefe

GRENELEFE, FLORIDA

*"54 holes
of the finest
uncrowded
golf courses
in the U.S."*

T he magic in the atmosphere here is in the feeling of relaxation. Guests return to enjoy their own grand adventures year after year, and we are no different.

Since we are golfers, we found our adventures on the 54 holes of the finest uncrowded golf courses in the U.S.

The West Course has been rated Number One by *Florida Golf Week,* and one of the Top 100 by *Golf Digest.* The 7,325-yard course has a championship rating of 74.2, and the South Course's 6,869 yards have a championship rating of 72.0.

Andy Bean, Grenelefe's touring pro, heads a golf instruction school if you should be interested. Debbie Austin, whom I had the privilege of playing with in the Dinah Shore at Palm Springs, makes her home at Grenelefe.

Accommodations are all villas of one and two bedrooms. The villas are all along the golf course fairways, and are complete with a full kitchen, living room, dining area, and master bedrooms.

As a resort guest, you can enjoy a "private lodge" atmosphere in the main buildings. Emphasis has been put on stone accents, cheerful skylights, and vaulted cedar ceilings. Grenelefe is a hidden jewel that shimmers with charm.

Other recreational adventures can be found in jogging, cycling, or boating on beautiful Lake Marion. There are four pools for swimming and a tennis complex rated among the Top 50 in the country by *Tennis Magazine.* (Grenelefe is the scene of the United Airlines' Tournament of Champions.) There are two large lakes with complete boat rental facilities if you like to fish.

Of course, fine dining is synonymous with Grenelefe. Try any of their three restaurants: the Grene Haron, Tuck's Table, or the Forest Pub.

You will find nightlife spice either at Top of Lefe Nightclub or at Tuck's most popular piano bar lounge.

Local attractions are Walt Disney World/Magic Kingdom/ EPCOT Center, Sea World, Circus World, and Kennedy Space Center.

The grand adventure of Grenelefe now includes enormous amounts of conference space. Soon, there will be a 16,000-square-foot Grand Ballroom.

As recipients of the Gold Key Award, Mobil's Four-Star Award, Four-Diamond Award, *Golf Digest's* Top 100 Golf Courses, and *Tennis Magazine's* Top 50 Tennis Resort award, Grenelefe has to be "premier."

The resort is conveniently located 40 minutes from Orlando. When you arrive, think of me; I'll be wishing to be with you.

From daylight to dusk, the magic in the atmosphere here offers a feeling of complete relaxation.

We found this to be an ideal retreat nestled on Sunset Mountain in the heart of the Smokies. It is a fine Resort Hotel and Country Club, with a staff dedicated to serving their guests. They made our stay a most relaxing and enriching experience.

Spacious guest accommodations feature warm, comfortable decor that reflects the hotel's friendly attitude. A number of suites are available if you prefer, with breathtaking views. At this writing, an expansion program is well underway, with a scheduled completion date of April, 1984, and an estimated cost of $17.4-million.

At present, there are 238 rooms in the Inn's main lodge and 22 rooms at the Country Club. Planned in the new expansion are a new 234,000-square-foot convention center plus 204 guest rooms on eight levels, all with panoramic views; a 120-seat specialty restaurant; nightclub garden court cocktail lounge; and an indoor/outdoor pool with enclosed terrace and pavilion.

This gracious hotel has been enjoyed by American presidents and European nobility since the turn of the century. Interestingly, I learned that the Country Club is much older than the Inn, which traces its heritage to the Swannonoa Hunt Club organized in 1893. For years, gracious hospitality and attentive service have been prized by their guests; and we were no different. Some of their first guests and regulars were Henry Ford, Harvey Firestone, and Thomas Edison.

Since 1893, a gracious hotel and golf club in the heart of the Smokies.

A great climate, clean air, and magnificent scenery, plus a terrific golf course enticed us to prolong our stay. Playing golf was so enjoyable because the course is so beautifully plush.

Though it does offer a challenge with the rolling fairways, this Carolina-style course is a Par 71. It will enchant you, for as far as you can see it is perfectly wooded.

With a course as gracious as the surroundings, it is apparent why nobility and others of prominence choose The Grove Park Inn and Country Club repeatedly for golf. It is hard to have a bad day on this course, where every green, fairway, and landscape is groomed to perfection.

The bill of fare is known throughout North Carolina for its abundant variety and quality. The elegant Plantation and Francis Marion Rooms provide full-course menu service during regular dining hours, while the Dogwood and Sunset Terrace offer full-service menus around the clock. For more intimate dining, the Country Club has both casual and elegant offerings.

Another plus for your perfect pleasure, they have a fully equipped health club.

Asheville enjoys excellent airline service to its modern jetport. Interstate Highways 26 and 40 intersect here, and it is an easy drive.

There are 15 other fine courses to play, all within one hour of the Grove Park. Tennis, hiking, rock-hounding, museums, and theatres await you. The world-renowned Biltmore House and Gardens, with its 250 rooms filled with priceless works of art, furniture, and antiques, is a terrific attraction. After your golf, it's a must to see!

"Gracious hospitality, attentive service, panoramic views"

Grove Park Inn
and Country Club

ASHEVILLE, NORTH CAROLINA

*Enjoys a
traditional
reputation*

*High
Hampton
Inn &
Country
Club*

CASHIERS, NORTH CAROLINA

This was the former home of the Hamptons of South Carolina, whose illustrious friends; including General Wade, used to visit, hunt, and come to relax. He eloquently loved this magnificent 2300 acre estate.

The next owners were internationally known. Dr. Halsted, head surgeon of John Hopkins and his wife, the former Caroline Hampton. After the Halsteds' death in 1922, High Hampton was acquired by the parents of the present owners.

Today it retains much of the tradition of the former era. The Inn and guest cottages blend with the natural beauty of the valley and the mountains, and the architecture has a mountain look.

The focal point in the lobby of the Inn is the four fireplaces, adding to a warm welcome. The rooms are rustic and comfortable, with sawmill finished pine and sturdy mountain crafted furniture. Golf cottages, two and three bedrooms, on the course are available.

If you can appreciate beautiful country cooking, you will love the country ham, cured and smoked to perfection, homemade breads and pastries, and even vegetables from their garden—American or European plans are offered.

The unique feature of this resort lies in the fact that commercialism hasn't touched the beauty. A perfect spot if you want R & R, serenity, and the beauty of nature. There are plenty of sporting options by day, but not many neon lights by night.

A par 71 18-hole course adjacent to the Inn was designed by George W. Cobb, internationally famous golf architect. His opinion is there are no courses he knows of with greater natural beauty, or that are more desirable to play anywhere. In addition to its scenic beauty, there are many lakes, plenty of ups and downs, and traps to challenge the good golfer.

Golf Digest has featured the 8th hole as one of America's great golf holes. It is a par 3, 137 yards, and plays to an island green amid stately trees and mountains. The scenery is actually a challenge: the lake, the tall hemlocks and white pines leave very little margin for error. The green drops off abruptly to the water at both front and back, so there could be some grief involved.

Other sporting options are tennis, trap and skeet shooting, horseback riding, water sports for swimmers and boaters, three lakes on the estate cover some 40 acres. Canoes, paddle boats and sailboats are available, too.

Fishing in their private lakes which are stocked by the Inn requires no license.

All seasons are particularly beautiful, but spring, summer and fall are probably the best. If you want to be 3,600 feet closer to Heaven than the sea, enjoy informal atmosphere and an unhurried pace, this could be the good life here.

The Homestead

HOT SPRINGS, VIRGINIA

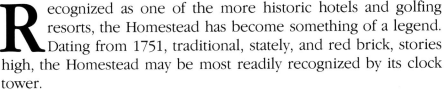

Recognized as one of the more historic hotels and golfing resorts, the Homestead has become something of a legend. Dating from 1751, traditional, stately, and red brick, stories high, the Homestead may be most readily recognized by its clock tower.

The moment you arrive at the doorsteps, uniformed attendants appear to greet you in the grand manner and serve your every need. Lodging accommodations vary from sitting rooms to gracious suites, all attractively decorated and comfortably furnished.

At ground level are a variety of exclusive shops, there to fill your leisure hours and offer the very thing you want or need.

The Homestead features three entirely separate and distinctive golf courses, each with its own identity, clubhouse, and pro. The Cascades (upper) was designed by William Flynn and built in 1923 about three miles from the Hotel. It is unquestionably one of America's finest and included by *Golf Digest* among "America's ten greatest tests of golf." The Lower Cascades (about six miles from the hotel) was designed by Robert Trent Jones and built in 1962 and is a real test for any golfer. However ageless Sam Snead tied the course record by carding a round of 60 at the age of 71. The Homestead course is the oldest and dates back to 1892. Situated adjacent to the Hotel, it is a 5,957-yard Par 71 reserved exclusively for Hotel guests.

The Homestead, at Hot Springs, Virginia, may be reached by auto or, if you wish, there is an airstrip for private planes. Should you choose to drive, we suggest you travel in April or May, particularly if you are a nature lover. No finer array of beautiful dogwoods and azaleas can be seen anywhere.

The twin traditions of the Homestead have been their sumptuous food and fine service. Should you seek a magnificent formal candlelight dinner and evening, you have something to look forward to! The main dining room at the Homestead possesses the unmistakable aura of elegance, with every appointment keyed to complement some very fine dining. There are fresh flowers at the table and each dish is served with style. Would you enjoy the dining style of the turn of the century? A cultured ambience? Then be transported back in time at the Homestead as you see your waiter approach your table with white gloves and impeccable attire. It is a rare experience anymore to be attended to like this. And, at the Homestead, it is quite apparent to you that these waiters seek to serve your every dining need. An astonishing variety of dinner dishes is available here and served only with class.

Here, too, for your enjoyment will be a fine orchestra, whether you choose to dance or merely to listen on into the night.

For a more casual meal, you may enjoy a tantalizing brunch or lunch. They claim to offer a menu of 1,500 different items. Now there *is* a temptation! We can personally attest to this!!!

Along with the fantastic golfing facilities, the visitor may also sample the riding horses, the tennis, and last but not least, one of the country's finest therapeutic bath clinics and mineral springs.

"Sumptuous food and fine service"

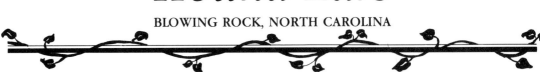

Hound Ears

BLOWING ROCK, NORTH CAROLINA

Tucked away in a valley of North Carolina's Blue Ridge Mountains is a complete resort facility with an intimate atmosphere. Hound Ears retains the charm and elegance of a private club. The resort is approximately 90 miles north of Charlotte, just off Highway 105 in Watauga County, at a height of 3,000 feet in the heart of the mountains.

Small and quaint, the lodge has only 25 rooms. However, 70 condominiums that surround the golf course, plus a number of homes built to follow the terrain of the mountain valleys are optional accommodations.

 The 18-hole golf course is the primary recreational amenity. George Cobb used the natural contours of the valley's streams and terrain as he ingeniously designed this 6,300-yard course for play. Recognized as a testy course, this charmer cannot be taken for granted as it is surrounded by total beauty. I can assure you that this is a course where your interests will be piqued.

Sporting two dining rooms, a lounge and other facilities, Hound Ears Club is widely known as being one of the finest dining establishments in America. Special emphasis is placed on their gourmet dinners.

Lodging is M.A.P. and the resort proudly displays Mobil Travel Guide's Four Star rating. Gentlemen are required to wear ties and coats after 6:30 p.m.

Aside from golf, there are facilities for tennis and swimming (the pool is built into a mountain grotto). In winter, skiing is popular. There are many side attractions such as hiking trails, riding stables, trout streams and lakes for canoeing and boating. Side trips to Grandfather Mountain, Tweetsie Railroad, and Blowing Rock are well worth the time.

I promise you that you will derive much pleasure from this unique resort's identity. By the way, the name comes from a local unique rock formation which hangs over the valley.

At left, 18th green is lush with flowers; above, view of the clubhouse and the ninth green. Your interest can easily be piqued in this setting of perfect, manicured beauty. But with waterholes, waterfalls, and small streams everywhere, don't feel too confident!

"The intimacy and elegance of a private club"

Hyatt Regency Grand Cypress

ORLANDO, FLORIDA

The 750 room luxury Hyatt Regency Grand Cypress, at Orlando, Florida is definitely a world-class resort destination.

The natural, tropical setting is further enhanced by a large area of land that has been left in the native state.

The lakes are stocked with native fish and natures flora and fauna left untouched literally. Plants, trees, lagoon-like setting with cascading waterfalls, natural greenery and jacuzzis among the rocks at waters edge is a real eye-full.

The guest rooms with 75 suites and VIP suites are multi-level and include a sleeping loft, private bar, spa and jacuzzi to mention a few special ammenities.

Their famous VIP European concierge service on the 11th floor, features a typical Florida feeling and is decorated with wicker furniture, ceiling fans, and shutters. Each room has a dramatic view of either the sprawling recreational areas or the elegant landscaped areas.

Three separate lounges include; the HURRICANE BAR and TRELLISE both featuring indoor and outdoor seating.

The White Horse Saloon is a themed entertainment lounge, and much fun can be had here.

Drinks are enjoyed at the Grotto Bar as well as at the Grand Cypress Golf Course. Four Restaurants make it a difficult choice as they are all superb.

La Coquina is a favored gourmet restaurant overlooking the lake. Hemingways, set on rocks overlooking the swimming pool, offers Key West flavor for steak and seafood, and is another favorite of their guests. The Cascade is the main dining room, featuring breakfast, lunch and dinner, offering ethnic Northern Italian cuisine...hard to beat....

The adjacent Terrace Restaurant features informal menus for guests in a hurry. Whatever ones tastebuds crave they will be amply satisfied here.

The Eques is a flashy showbar "the in place for the crowd over 25."

Along with this GRAND RESORT the Jack Nicklaus signature golf course, has the look and feel of St. Andrews. A perfect course for proving yourself against your game. An extremely interesting, and definitely challenging course it is 7,054 yards long and is a par 72.

Multi levels and tiers add to the flavor, along with adding extra difficulty. Visually exciting, the course features grassy dunes, natural brush-like hazards, pot bunkers and wildflowers.

The course is opened exclusively to the hotel guests.

The nine hole pitch and putt is a complement to the 18 hole, and is a great place for readying one self for the real McCoy.

Besides the golf other recreational activities include a half-acre free form swimming pool with 12 water falls, 3 jacuzzis, a 45 foot water slide and grotto bar.

A 21 acre lake with a marina and sailboats, windsurfers, canoes, and paddleboats; a tennis recreational complex, plus Grand Cypress Racquet Club are other sporting options, along with racquetball and shuffleboard courts there is a complete Health Club and Spa with separate facilities.

As if this is not enough they have grand facilities for conferences and can accommodate groups of differing sizes.

Close to many choice tourist spots, don't miss this one...a great choice.

*A world-class
resort destination.*

Hyatt On Hilton Head Island at Palmetto Dunes

HILTON HEAD ISLAND, SOUTH CAROLINA

The Hyatt on Hilton Head Island is one of the southeast's largest resorts. Bordered by a three mile stretch of sand beach along the Atlantic, it rises gracefully against a backdrop of majestic oaks. In the heart of Palmetto Dunes Resort it is surrounded by golf, tennis and every conceivable sport for year round activity.

There are 519 luxurious rooms and suites, including fourteen sunset suites, four oceanfront hospitality suites, six executive suites and two oceanfront presidential suites with up to four bedrooms. All accommodations are richly decorated in the Hyatt tradition, and every amenity will await you.

For your dining pleasure, there is Hugo's Bar and Seafood Grille, famous for its casual elegance and fabulous food, or for a casual snack you can go poolside to the Possum Point. A beautiful new gourmet room has recently been added and will be a culinary high spot of your visit. Also the new poolside restaurant will do great things for your tastebuds. For late night activities the hot spot is Club Indigo.

"One of the brightest stars in the Hilton Head constellation of four-star oceanfront hostelries."

Just outside the hotel are two championship golf courses, and the third will be completed in 1986. These magnificent courses were designed by the famous George Fazio and Robert Trent Jones. If you want a challenge, I can attest there can be plenty here. In their typical manner of design, there are loads of sand bunkers, plenty of water, and undulated fairways. Your work will be cut out for you....

They are all championship calibre courses and do demand some skills but then, of course, a little luck never hurts anyone—right???

The Hills Course is opening 1986, designed by Arthur Hills. The Robert Trent Jones course measures 6,707 yards; the 10th hole goes to the ocean, and is quite a sight. The Fazio course measures 6,873 yards long—the holes run parallel and it has loads of sand and has been listed by Golf Digest as one of America's 100 best.

If you are a tennis buff, Rod Laver welcomes you to the Rod Laver Center. There are 25 courts in two well-planned complexes. Several are lighted for night play.

Some of the new harbour-view villas in Shelter Cove offer private jacuzzis. All villas are handsomely furnished and completely equipped. You may choose from one to four bedroom villas or even luxurious private homes.

Shelter Cove offers quayside dining and shopping. Whatever you're looking for, you should be able to find it here.

Innisbrook

TARPON SPRINGS, FLORIDA

H ere are 63 holes of golf in a setting nature created especially for you. When we arrived at this resort, we knew immediately that it was one of Florida's "Premiers." This resort is nestled in tall, ancient pines with mossy beards, azaleas and hibiscus, graced with the golden sun and endowed with gentle breezes.

Each individual suite is a privately-owned condominium home, richly but comfortably decorated.

"63 holes of golf especially for you"

Awaiting Innisbrook's guests are three championship golf courses. One of the layouts is the Island Course, which has been voted the "Most Interesting" course in Florida by a panel of state golf professionals and writers. Styled with beauty and grace, it is a challenging 7,000 yards.

The Copperhead Course, which can be as deadly as its namesake, has been rated among the "Top 100" courses in America by *Golf Digest* and in Florida's *Golfweek Magazine* as one of the state's "Top 50." The Copperhead Course offers variety in its 27 holes and in its 6,800 to 7,000 yards (depending on which combination of nines are played).

The real test of your game can be Innisbrook's 18-hole Sandpiper Course. Only 6,087 yards, it is short, but it demands concentration and accuracy. A recommendation for players of all abilities: many water hazards are accented with wild birds of all descriptions. Unusual in a Florida course, Innisbrook's fairways are lush and have carefully manicured greens. Strategically placed water hazards and gaping sand bunkers offer beauty but challenge.

Fairways ramble uphill and downhill throughout 1,000 acres, adding an extra dimension to your golfing enjoyment.

For your culinary curiosities, a range of restaurants offers variety to match your mood. You can't beat the chandeliered Regency Room for gourmet cuisine served in superb style with impeccable service.

If you are activity-prone, you will find the Island Clubhouse a very likeable spot. It houses the Vintage Room and the Terrace Garden. Each is distinctively decorated and carries through with the ambience suggested by its name. The Copperhead Clubhouses feature a nightclub and dining room with two shows nightly. At the Sandpiper, you get a breathtaking view of the golf course and of dozens of herons, egrets, mallards, and white geese.

Daytime golfers may revive at the La Mancha Lounge, which also has entertainment nightly.

Innisbrook has won a number of awards for standards of excellence while retaining all the splendor of the natural landscape and design. It is recognized with a World Tennis Five Star designation for excellence in facilities and instructors. It also features 60 acres of lakes and five swimming pools. A complete health club offers the latest equipment and a supervised fitness program.

Located between Clearwater, Florida, and Tarpon Springs, this modern day award-winning legend is truly a winner.

Innisbrook

Hotel Inter·Continental at Port Royal Resort

HILTON HEAD, SOUTH CAROLINA

Located on twenty-four acres within Pt. Royal and situated on an 18 acre beachfront site facing the Atlantic Ocean, this seaside resort is reminiscent of a bygone era. The architectural design harkens to the Southern heritage of Charleston and Savannah. Throughout the central courtyard are pools, fountains and lush tropical landscaping.

The redwood poolside deck affords the sight and sounds of the ocean just steps away. The five-story building provides ocean views for all 416 guest rooms with every amenity you could expect from a luxury hotel. Colorfully and tastefully decorated, the rooms are furnished to capture the elegance and informality of the island.

Inter-Continental Hotels are famous for distinctive dining and excellent service, and dining here will certainly be no different. The hotel's elegant Specialty Restaurant, the Barony, is furnished in country French decor with rich wood, traditional fabrics, beamed ceilings and beveled glass French windows facing the gardens. Impeccable international cuisine or delightful local specialties will be yours to enjoy.

The Brasserie for all-day dining is decorated in bright, crisp decor. Also outdoor dining here on the terrace enables one to enjoy the balmy breezes and beautiful views. Poolside you may opt for the Playful Pelican.

The Gazebo is perfect for conversation and cocktails. For cocktail time you can relax in the Lobby Lounge adjacent to or on the veranda. A recreation of an old elegant Southern home, where you will be accompanied by the sounds of the Atlantic Ocean only a few steps away.

Prevailing in the evening for your entertainment, music and dancing can top off a perfect evening. Last but not least, the Beach Club Area is festive for barbecues.

The Marsh Tacky, named for the original watering hole, offers the best of the island. Exotic beverages and live beach music with the Atlantic Ocean as the backdrop offer an informal and relaxed attitude.

Situated on an 18-acre beachfront in the beautiful Port Royal Plantation.

On the island there are 18 golf courses, and at Inter-Continental at Pt. Royal you are offered three 18-hole par 72 golf courses. The Barony is 6,530 yards long. Planter's Row is 6520 yards long and is a brand new one. Robber's Row, is 6711 yards long and either will challenge your handicap from any tee.

This year Port Royal Golf Club will proudly host a major Seniors PGA Tour tournament. The greens are undulated and winding streams come into play. The pine tree-lined rolling fairways are as challenging as they are pretty. Besides all this, they are impeccably maintained and superbly designed.

You may play Shipyard, too, as guests of the Inter-Continental.

They have just introduced a new racquet club, there are three Grand Slam Court surfaces and 16 championship tennis courts.

Racquetball courts, a beautiful health club plus indoor and outdoor swimming pools are all within this peaceful and quiet ocean-swept locale. If you elect to stay in one of the 300 1- and 2-bedroom villas, they are all luxurious. Elegant home rentals are available if you should want more privacy.

Kiawah

CHARLESTON,
SOUTH CAROLINA

"A complete resort in complete harmony with nature"

Designed in complete harmony with nature, this quiet luxurious place can soothe you. Situated on a 10,000-acre, semi-tropical sea island, it is coming on strong for the avid golfer. The thing that is great about this place is that once you're there, you don't even need your car as everything is compact in the layout of the resort.

Accommodations consist of four separate lodges, cottages, and villas. Each guest is pampered in rooms with balconies overlooking the ocean, the pool, or a lagoon in a wooded landscape.

Though the atmosphere is casual, Kiawah will capture your fancy with simple gestures such as your morning paper, hot coffee, and mints on your pillow for sweet dreams.

Kiawah is a golfer's paradise with three 18-hole golf courses, each with its own personality and challenge.

The Turtle Point Golf Club was designed by Jack Nicklaus. It is 6,889 yards, a Par 72. The three spectacular holes on the oceanfront, the fairways, and the greenside bunkers are the closest thing to Scotland you will find.

The original Kiawah Links were designed by Gary Player. It is a Par 71, championship layout. The wide tee shot landing areas and small greens make it an ideal course. Though it is only 6,250 yards, it challenges you as it wanders through lagoons, palmettos, and forests of live oak trees.

Yet another course is under construction at this time. It is being designed by Tom Fazio. How can you miss with such a combination of designing architects? Tom Fazio promises that this course will be challenging for the low handicapper, but weekend golfers will enjoy it, too.

An array of choices for your palate consists of very casual to continental cuisine. Especially regal with classic continental cuisine, the Charleston Gallery French Restaurant will be quietly soothing. The Jasmine Porch is the island's flagship restaurant, serving breakfast, lunch, and dinner and their famous Sunday brunch.

On mild days the Jasmine Veranda is a hub. Several additional alternatives are available at the Straw Market or at Jonah's Last Straw. The Sand Wedge serves snacks and drinks for golfers. Be sure to have some of the "She Crab Soup" at the Jasmine Porch. It really is good.

Tennis, biking, shelling, jeep safaris, landsailing, beachcombing, and fishing cannot be overlooked.

After your day packed full of pleasure, you have one more surprise to look forward to, and that is the spa, complete with a whirlpool. Swimming is popular here, and what a setting, as the pool is beachside.

Air travel to Charleston International Airport is convenient from anywhere in the country. Limousine service is scheduled for Kiawah's guests, or if you prefer you may rent a car. It is a nice drive.

Above, ocean holes #14, #15, and #16 at Turtle Point Golf Club Left, hole #5 at Marsh Point Golf Club.

Golf pro shop is located behind this landmark.

Lexington Marriott Resort Griffin Gate

LEXINGTON, KENTUCKY

The word "Kentucky" has the ring of "horses" to it, but imagine turning off a modern highway and entering a spectacular hotel with dramatic atriums, waterfalls, and fountains right square in the middle of all this lush horse country. It truly is something you would not envision unless you had shared such an experience.

Sprawling completely around the property are some of the richest horse farms in the world. Expansive, spotlessly white fences and verdant grazing land complement the foliage in this memorable setting. Your sudden awareness of the resort states "lavishness." Accommodations are richly done and include many amenities you would expect to find only at home.

Next, an astonishing variety of culinary styles awaits you. Traditional favorites are enhanced in the setting of the Griffin Gate Gardens, located in a soaring atrium. To be exact, it is the waterfalls which "soar" in this extraordinary setting, with many ficus trees and rich warm-colored plants, all dominantly overlooking the golf course. A few steps away is the Pegasus Lounge, supposedly one of Lexington's "in" spots. We could well understand its popularity. Pegasus offers dancing and backgammon as well as generous cocktails. Later, we enjoyed the Oyster Bar, which serves all-fresh clams, shrimps, and oysters (in season).

Yet another bar, The Lobby, is a choice night spot to visit before retiring for the evening. Located in a charming gazebo, The Lobby has a clock tower as its focal point and a pianist for its nightly entertainment, with guests often joining in. During golf, or afterwards, the Snack Shop offers many of the day's tempting selections.

Speaking of golf, this challenging 18 holes is a Rees Jones design and is over 6,800 yards long, comprised of undulating greens plus 64 huge sand traps. Water comes into play on 12 of the 18 holes. Though a fairly new course, it is not new by comparison as it is surrounded by mature trees and greenery.

Other sports include tennis, lighted for night, and swimming if you are so inclined, either in the outdoor pool or the indoor pool. The latter offers a blissful experience and is one of the resort's favorite gathering places. Sunworshippers will find large sunbathing decks, and to fit anyone's fancy — guess what? — the Lexington Marriott offers a superb health club complete with exercise rooms, saunas, and hydrotherapy pool. If you are competitively spirited, a game room awaits you, filled with electronic wonders.

Should you be planning a program or conference, you will find outstanding meeting features, framed by the Marriott's legendary expertise, assuring spontaneous combustion for any event you choose to bring to this remarkable setting.

Located less than 15 minutes from Lexington's Blue Grass Field Airport and close to both Keeneland Race Course and Red Mile Race Track, this resort offers a multitude of extracurricular activities. If you plan well in advance, imagine the thrill of attending the Kentucky Derby! When you're looking for a blue grass winner, go with the Lexington Marriott Resort Griffin Gate. You will thank me.

"When you think Blue Grass Country, go with a winner"

Course is characterized by large undulating greens with five different tee elevations per hole. As if this weren't enough, water comes into play on 12 of the 18 holes!!!

Discover a wealth of pleasures and activities on Florida's Gulf Coast.

A wealth of pleasures and activities await your discovery on Florida's Gulf Coast. Accommodations are privately owned and individually decorated for their guests. Luxury is the key and every selection has been discriminately chosen—the same as having your own, but less worry and work.

Being a "premiere" personal resort, it has been tucked into a secluded island surrounded by resort amenities and carefully blended with elegant tropical homes, on recreational pursuits and lush Florida foliage. A hallmark of service and outstanding food will make your stay superb.

At sunset the Orchid Room is breathtaking and the continental cuisine is graciously prepared and served. You will love the attention as they really care about your needs.

LeClub in Island House is a perfect place for dinner or a nightcap, and afterwards take a stroll on the manicured grounds or you can walk on the beach.

Thirty-six championship golf holes assure you of the perfect golfing holiday, offering you a challenge to your skills while affording you some of the most spectacular views of the island and the Gulf of Mexico.

Much water, well-trapped bunkers, plus a lot of scenic beauty make it a must for concentrating.

Knowledgeable golfers return repeatedly and it is a desirable place for tournaments. Harbourside is 6,783 yards long, while the Islandside Golf Course, another 18 hole championship course, is just under 7,000 yards long. The golf club also boasts a fine dining room and cocktail lounge overlooking the Islandside Golf Course.

The climate of Longboat Key has been compared to that of the Mediterranean's Riviera with an average temperature of 71 degrees—how could you miss?

For tennis lovers, Longboat Key offers 20 meticulously-maintained Har-Tru Courts for fun and sport. Sailing and boating at the Harbourside, plus a spectacular pool for your swimming pleasure, will only add to your sporting vacation.

A place to truly be pampered without a tuxedo. With a special at-home feeling ambience, in one of the few world class resorts, will assure a return visit.

Also for you tennis buffs an Islandside Tennis Center incorporates fourteen Har-tru tennis courts on the Gulfs edge, equipped with a pro and tennis pro shop.

For the beachcomber you have the unspoiled, unhurried, perfect beach facility to really enjoy.

Longboat Key Club

LONGBOAT KEY, FLORIDA

John Ringling the "Circus King" had a dream, which the Arvida Corporation fulfilled with the building of the famous Ritz Carlton at Sarasota, but because of his all-or-nothing spirit the Inn on the Beach at Longboat Key Club was built, and is certainly a proud successor on this celebrated site.

Marriott's Grand Hotel

POINT CLEAR, ALABAMA

It is no wonder that this beautifully situated hotel is called the "Queen of Southern Resorts." It will be evident to you, too, when you arrive at Point Clear, Alabama, located on the Gulf Coast, that you are at a premier golf resort. You will discover the complete luxury of today, but with the hospitality and traditional charm of the Old South.

Immediately upon your arrival, you are intrigued by the service yet you feel a quiet ambience, assuring you that the "grand manner of excellence" is alive today. A staff of 400 is waiting to cater to your every need.

For golf, their nationally-known Lakewood Club is a complete club in itself. It features 27 holes on three nine-hole courses: the Azalea, the Dogwood, and the Magnolia. It has been said that playing these courses alone can be a mystical experience to any golfer.

Besides being ranked as a unique layout, it is one of the very few courses you can play that does not require a tee time. Playing is a delight as you can play undistracted in a quiet, unhurried, and uncrowded atmosphere. How long has it been since you have played without a tee time?

Magnolias, dogwoods, and azaleas elaborately accent the fairways, along with lush greenery. By any standard, it is a pretty but special golfing experience.

Loads of trees are just waiting to welcome you, along with sand and water and narrow fairways. At this writing, it is my understanding that along with the extensive remodelling of the hotel, much emphasis is being put into the golf courses as another target for beautification.

Accommodations are offered in "grand style" with a choice of the main hotel, the bay house, or cottages. All of these have been refurbished.

Privileged to stay in a freshly re-done suite, it was evident that luxury is their standard. Every amenity of home is carefully provided, along with the visual beauty and comfort they have adopted for their guests' enjoyment.

Over the years, the Grand Hotel has had a following of repeat guests, making it a very friendly place. For early risers, coffee is served each morning in the lobby where everyone gathers and chats.

For breakfast and lunch, a Southern dining room enhances the presentation of their Southern cookery. If you crave a little more fun and activity, the Bird Cage Lounge, overlooking the sparkling bay, offers a commanding view and some exciting nightlife as well.

Tennis courts are available. If you care for boating, they have a private marina. Maybe you would like to change your pace and try your luck at deep sea fishing or water-skiing. Perhaps a swim at the sprawling pool or a dip in Mobile Bay. Whatever your interest, the facilities are excellent.

Ground transportation can be arranged from Fairhope Airport, five miles from the hotel. Limousines will meet your plane on request.

A sincere opinion—this aristocratic grand Southern resort commands applause.

"Queen of the Southern resorts"

Mission Inn

HOWEY-IN-THE-HILLS, FLORIDA

H illy fairways and velvet greens, massive oaks and spring-fed lakes blending with classic architecture create a warmth and magic of a Spanish hacienda. Reigning as one of Florida's premier resorts it is "one-of-a-kind and offers a tradition of luxury and first-class service."

As a family run resort their commitment to excellence has earned them a Mobil Four Star Travel Award consecutively since 1977. Guests may choose from a variety of accommodations: Luxury suites with one or two bedrooms, living room, wet bar and private balconies. Enchanting villas or plush hotel rooms furnished in authentic Spanish decor reminiscent of the mission era.

The Vista Patio offers quick lunches and snacks.

La Riena is a classic 1930's River Yacht. She was restored in 1984 to her original lustre and elegance. You can enjoy panoramic views of sparkling Lake Harris as you set out for a sunset cruise, reception or brunch. Dining will be a highlight of your stay—The El Conquistador dining room serves Florida specialties.

Cocktails, entertainment and dancing are featured in the delightful El Bodegon lounge.

A world of Tennis "Five Star," they have six Laykold tennis courts, exercise rooms and jogging trails, swimming and Hydro-Spa, shuffleboard and volleyball, playground and gameroom plus a Fitness Center.

If you haven't been to Howey in the hills—go now. The excellent 18-hole championship golf course provides a unique challenge to this hilly region of the state. Pine trees guard winding fairways that slope with the rolling hills, accented with clear lakes enhanced by red tile roofs, archways, and lush greenery. It is a golfer's delight, all 6,858 yards. Of the 800 Florida courses this one ranks 17th best! Every lie is a surpise uphill, downhill, and sidehill. On the front nine there is water on every hole. Recognized as one of the ten toughest courses in the state of Florida, trees, towering old pines and oaks line the fairways. Don't be surprised if you see an alligator resting on the shores of a water hole, or gliding on the lakes.

The #4 546 yard, par 5 has acquired the title of "The Devil's Delight," because of the numerous obstacles.

Next time your planning an unusually quiet, but exciting golfing vacation, the Mission Inn can be your great "ESCAPE."

"Not just another resort, but a plush, private estate."
Mission Inn reigns over Florida's most beautiful terrain in
a setting which befits a premier resort.

A family run resort
their commitment
is for excellence "A
Mobil Four Star
Travel Award"

The lobby, above, beckons guests for peaceful relaxation at Myrtle Beach, where life is as soft and easy as the ocean breezes.

I f you yearn for a vacation by the sea, have I got a place for you! Making this resort unique is the fact that it is the only hotel in Myrtle Beach with its own private golf course. For years, we have given preference to the Hilton chain when we travel, since their service and surroundings are hard to beat. This particular hotel is located on the Grand Strand of South Carolina, where life is as soft and easy as the ocean breezes.

The lobby is casual but elegant, decorated in impeccably chosen colors, fabrics, and furnishings selected to please their guests. Sunshine by day, bright lights by night; or you may find solitude and quiet moments if you prefer.

Myrtle Beach Hilton

**MYRTLE BEACH,
SOUTH CAROLINA**

When you think of Myrtle Beach, immediately you think of golf.

At this time, I am told that there are 35 golf courses in the area. When you are a guest at the Hilton, you are eligible to play the Hilton's course plus most of the other ones. All you need do is obtain a guest pass and pay your green fees.

The Grand Strand has earned its nickname of "Golf Supermarket." Nowhere else in the country can you find this many golf courses in such a variety of championship classes. One has to be reached by cable car, and another has an alligator hazard.

Their beautiful 6,950-acre Arcadian Shores Golf Club is right outside your door when you are the Hilton's guest. Designed by Rees Jones, it has been listed as one of the top 100 by *Golf Digest.* Arcadian is a challenge for golfers at any level. Offering much water and many trees, it makes a picturesque statement. It has also earned recognition for an outstanding pro shop which has a plentiful supply of fashionable necessities and captivating collectibles.

"When you think of Myrtle Beach, you think of golf"

Continental cuisine is featured nightly at Alfredo's, with a view almost as spectacular as the food. Everything here is served in a plush atmosphere, richly furnished — an almost perfect environment. My sincere compliments went to the chef the night we were there, as the food was absolutely a gourmet's delight. To add to our pleasure, there were flickering candles, superb settings, floral arrangements, and distinctive service.

Another World, located on top of the hotel, is Myrtle Beach's most unique entertainment center and a very "in" place. Specialty buffets on the beach are legendary, and for tiny appetites there is the coffee shop or the pool terrace.

An Olympic-size pool is strategically located with the Atlantic Ocean as its immediate neighbor. Tennis, sailing, an outing on a catamaran, or just a stroll on the beach can complete your day in a splendiferous way.

Try it, you will like it.

Palm Beach Polo and Country Club

WEST PALM BEACH, FLORIDA

S ituated in the upper portion of Florida's Gold Coast, less than 10 miles from West Palm Beach, this premier resort is located at Wellington, one of South Florida's newest and most beautiful communities. It sits on 1,650 acres and ranks among the world's most prestigious resort complexes.

Resort accommodations are available in privately-owned villas and lodges; or you may choose between the lodge (located in the Golf and Tennis Village) and guest facilities in the Polo Village. Luxurious manors and distinctive residences are yet another option in a setting of aristocratic excellence. You must see it for yourself.

The Palm Beach Country Club is known for exclusive restaurants featuring seafood, steak, and house specialties. The dining rooms will let you opt for a formal or cozy evening; or for a more laid-back stance, you can settle in the Casual Players Club. Both offer entertainment.

A delightful blend of counts, cowboys, princesses, playboys, and golfers, living life to the hilt.

Two golf courses dominate the Golf and Tennis Village. The first 18-hole championship course — home of many tournaments — was designed by George Fazio, and it provides much diversion while stretching over 6,715 yards. It is reserved exclusively for members and guests. Scheduled for completion in 1984, the new 18-holes, planned by Ron Garl and Associates and Jerry Pate, will be Scottish in character and will utilize sand dunes with native vegetation, including sea oats and grasses. Apparently, there will be "nothing like it in the area." You will also have the use of a new clubhouse, restaurant and bar, plus a pro shop.

"Club Sporting Annex is unparalleled"

The Club's sporting annex is unparalleled, with the John Gardiner Tennis Center forming the hub of activity. Within the confines, you will find complete equestrian facilities, and polo has literally been the annex's "middle name." Here the world gathers to watch the best the sport has to offer. A delightful blend of counts, cowboys, princesses, and playboys — living life to the hilt — adds a spirited ambience to the Club. Along with them, you can "live it up," for Palm Beach Polo and Country Club surely has it all.

P.G.A. National Golf Club at the P.G.A. Sheraton Resort

PALM BEACH GARDENS, FLORIDA

"A Shangri-La for Golf"

This expansive resort, with its perpetual sunshine, is plush indeed. The moment you check in, you feel the ambience of a spacious, uncrowded sports haven. Sheraton has incorporated style, decor, warmth, and most of all, the comforts of home.

A quiet, understated elegance permeates the atmosphere as you enjoy your guest room, where architects and decorators have spared nothing, creating luxury in depth, with a bright, cheerful Palm Beach motif. And the furnishings are every bit as comfortable as they are attractive.

Each guest has a private balcony that overlooks the golf course, the lake, or a courtyard, and there are 336 rooms for you to choose from.

The P.G.A. Sheraton is an oasis for fine food and beverages. You may select the Explorers Club, with an ongoing menu and atmosphere to match. Colonel Bogey's, a favorite of many, serves steaks and chops. Their chicken done on an open rotisserie is fun to watch and good to eat. The Citrus Tree is an indoor-outdoor terrace overlooking the pool, serving breakfast, lunch, and dinner.

For your 19th hole, favorite thirst quenchers can be found at the Legends. A special entertainment center presents music for dancing and listening or just mixing with friends, and it is comfortably located.

Speaking of locations, once the avid golfer finds this one, he feels he has found a small piece of heaven with four championship courses to choose from. The Haig, designed by the celebrated team of Tom and George Fazio, is a 6,973-yard, Par 72 course that can be played by any golfer. It is an excellent driving course and invites all handicaps.

The Champion, also a Fazio, is typically Scottish in design. It is a challenging 7,137-yard, Par 72 with over 100 bunkers and 16 water holes. The Squire, a third Fazio course, is 6,800 yards and a Par 72. Considered to be "the thinking man's course," it forces the player to place shots if he wants to score.

The General, now being designed by Arnold Palmer, will be 7,000 yards and a Par 72. This course will open early in 1984 and will feature St. Andrews double greens and, of course, the level change and beauty that Arnold Palmer brings out in his courses.

The 1983 Ryder Cup matches will be held here and the international visitors are sure to be pleased.

Besides your Shangri-la for golf, if you are into tennis, they have plenty of that, too, along with a 26-acre lake where you may enjoy paddleboating or sailing. They have stations for jogging and hiking and a 40-acre wilderness preserve. Nearby is horseback riding and sportfishing. Two swimming pools are ready to refresh you, and a lot of fun awaits your shopping in the hotel. For further shopping adventures, you're not too far from the world-famous Worth Avenue.

Located on P.G.A. Boulevard just off the Florida Turnpike Exit 44, this elegant sports center is 15 miles north of West Palm Beach International Airport.

P.S. I almost forgot to mention that the P.G.A. of America has a new home at the entrance of the P.G.A. National resort community. This is something no serious golfer will want to miss.

"If you're looking for championship everything, they have it all including a complete fitness center"

PineIsle

LAKE LANIER, GEORGIA

Just 45 minutes from Atlanta is a Stouffer resort on 38,000-acre Lake Lanier. Here you will find tranquility you've only imagined before. As we drove around the Lake Lanier Islands, pine-studded, miles and miles of unspoiled shoreline were revealed to our wondering eyes. It's a perfect setting with a unique blend of beach and forest.

Every thought has been put into assuring your comfort as PineIsle's guest. Awaiting you are 250 spacious and newly decorated guest rooms and suites. From the moment you arrive, attendants are at your service.

If you've forgotten any of your toiletries, shampoo, or other personal items, don't worry. These items will be in your complimen-

tary basket. A basket of fruit and lovely wine was added to make our stay festive.

When you're ready for golf, you'll have a real challenge on their 18-hole championship course, co-designed by Gary Player and Ron Kirby and Associates. Tight fairways constantly test your skills with multi-tiered greens and numerous water hazards. It was a real pleasure for us to meet Tommy Aaron, winner of the 1973 Masters Golf Tournament, currently the Director of Golf and Sales Promotion Department at PineIsle. We enjoyed chatting and comparing golf stories with this real gentleman. He reassured me that it was not particularly my game that was in trouble that day; even the pros feel that this course is slightly unforgiving.

Dining opportunities vary from informal snacks poolside at the Marina Grill to a most elegant experience of fine continental cuisine in the Pavilion. Try relaxing at the Gazebo, with a never-ending view of the lake. After dark, Sidney's is where the excitement is with music from a quiet piano or a live band.

The hotel staff doesn't rest on its laurels. In their continuing effort to keep PineIsle at the forefront of Southeastern resorts, the staff and management focus on constantly improving the resort, keeping their guests Number One.

A variety of activities is available within the Lake Lanier Islands, including horseback riding, sailing, waterskiing, professional guided fishing, tennis, and of course, simple relaxation.

Peaceful surroundings and golfing challenge combine on PineIsle's championship course. Aquatic sports flourish here, too, among the miles of beautiful shoreline.

"Tranquility you've only imagined"

Amid stately pines and colorful blossoms, this premier golf resort has been favored for over 80 years by golfers from all over the world. It is still as *grande* today and bears a reputation for friendly and exceptional service, with the quiet grace and charm of a bygone era. Pinehurst is a major vacation destination, and guests congregate here from all over the world.

A variety of accommodations are available, from one of the 310 luxurious rooms in the hotel to four-bedroom villas or two- or three-bedroom condominiums — and to add to that selection, you may even opt for a treehouse, some with full kitchens that may be rented from one day to a month.

A true golfer's paradise, Pinehurst is known as the "Golf Capital of the World." There are six courses to choose from. Number One has been redesigned by Donald Ross and bears little resemblance to the course that was originally built in 1898–1899 by Dr. LeRoy Culver. Though this course is short, it makes up for its length with its tight and tricky fairways. Trees and often rolling fairways require you to use every club in your bag.

Number Two is considered the best effort of Donald Ross and has been selected as one of the top courses in the world. This course features small, sloping greens, deep bunkers, loose sandy soil, and the rough called "love grass" (but that's not what I call it!). Fairways are deceptive, but wide, and the course has often been described as one of the most difficult courses in the world. A very popular course with any golfer, Number Two has been host to many tournaments.

Number Three has the greatest variety of design. Holes are in forested and hilly terrain which somewhat resembles a Scottish setting. Two of the Par 3's are a bit more than 200 yards, and the trickiest of all is the 9th hole at 175 yards, playing to a tiny, sloping green.

Number Four has undergone several facelifts, but the gentle swales and undulating greens, along with artfully placed bunkers, add to its strength and beauty. Water, sand, and trees offer quite a test of your skill. Hole #12 is 520 yards downhill and over water; it becomes quite a teaser.

Number Five Course has been worked and reworked many times, and now is supposed to be second to hardest of the six. It is long and very demanding and offers more water holes than any other.

Number Six, the latest addition, designed by George and Tom Fazio, is three miles from the main clubhouse and presents a setting with a different mood. Rolling hills, oaks, and pines beckon, but forget your errant shots.

All the greats of golf have played and are still playing in this "Golf Capital." Now it can be your turn.

Pinehurst Hotel and Country Club

PINEHURST, NORTH CAROLINA

After winding down from your day on the links, Pinehurst has some appealing options. Eating is synonymous with golf here, and you can't miss in the Carolina Room if you like Continental cuisine and just plain good food with candlelight, music, flowers, and perfect atmosphere. For your more casual desires, the London Grill is a warm, intimate spot where the service and food cannot be improved upon.

Tennis is big here, as is horseback riding, boating on their 200-acre lake, or just relaxing and sunning on the beach.

The quaint village just a stroll from the hotel is a place where "time stands still," and shopping and checking out its restaurants provide happy occasions.

While you're at Pinehurst, don't forget to see the World's Golf Hall of Fame. It'll be a special treat for you as a golfer.

"Six great courses — called 'Golf Capital of the World'"

Sawgrass

"The marine influence here is pervasive"

Sawgrass

PONTE VEDRA BEACH, FLORIDA

I n north Florida, midway between Jacksonville and St. Augustine, you will find one of the most serene, yet easily accessible, of all golf resorts — Sawgrass.

The marine influence here is pervasive, from the sounds of waves rolling up the shorefront at Ponte Vedra Beach to the calls of waterfowl in the Sawgrass Wilderness Preserve. And there is the fresh smell of Atlantic sea breezes blowing gently across three spectacular golf courses which feature fresh water as an integral part of all 54 holes. Natural woods blend harmoniously with lush golf fairways, sparkling lakes, and stands of palmettos.

Another attraction to Sawgrass is the Tournament Players' Club Course designed by Pete Dye. It has become the permanent home of the Tournament Players' Association, and the championship is held each March. Par is 72 on this course, and with four tees on every hole, average golfers (with some well-placed strokes) can be within reach of par. The full championship distance is 6,857 yards, but by using the front tees, the course can be shortened to 5,034 yards. This has to be one of the most "unique" golf courses ever to be designed. When you first look at it, it looks like a nightmare, but later you realize it is a challenge and great fun.

Sawgrass also offers championship play on its Oceanside Course, formerly used by the TPA Tour Championship, and on its newly-renovated Oak Bridge Course that is a full 6,109 yards.

Unlike many Florida courses that are unrelievedly flat, Sawgrass' courses are sculpted with cutouts, mounds, and swales.

Accommodations at Sawgrass are elegant, yet comfortable. Guests are lodged in completely furnished beach studios or in privately owned two, three, or four-bedroom luxury villas supplied with all the amenities of home.

Arvida Resorts, corporate owners of Sawgrass, pride themselves on their excellent food and impeccable service. The Beach Club, which overlooks the Atlantic Ocean, offers a wide selection of European and regional specialties prepared under the supervision of Sawgrass' French-trained chef. Dinner jackets for the men are *de rigueur,* but daytime dining is more casual.

Aside from exciting golf and satisfying dining, Sawgrass offers other diversions including hiking and biking along nature trails. It also boasts 13 professional clay tennis courts at the Racquet Club, and an excellent choice of horses is available for equestrians.

For children, Sawgrass maintains a year-round activities staff to ensure as pleasant a holiday for the youngsters as for their parents.

Prime time for a retreat to Sawgrass to enjoy their many outdoor activities is in the spring or fall when the temperatures hover in the mid-70's. But my husband and I love it so much any time suits us just fine.

Sea Pines Plantation

HILTON HEAD ISLAND, SOUTH CAROLINA

Home of the famous Heritage Classic

Today Sea Pines is vibrant, exciting, relaxing and enjoyable. Visitors enjoy the peace and quiet, plus the romantic escape.

The Harbour Town is certainly an activity center of Hilton Head. The Marina, shops, restaurants, lounges and conference facilities make this a most famous spot. Many of the homes have fairway and lagoon views, some with private pools.

The Plantation Club, centrally located in a country club setting, offers restaurant, swimming pools, and conference facilities.

Accommodations cluster in small groups of condominiums close to the excitement and activities of the Plantation's central meeting place. Just steps away from the Plantation Club is the private Sea Pines Beach Club, an ever popular gathering spot for beachside fun.

South Beach, a New England style village with marina, restaurants, swimming pools, and a marina store, plus 13 court Racquet Club, offers homes with an ocean view within feet of the Atlantic. Accommodations range from fully furnished housekeeping rooms equipped with all the amenities of home, completely charming, and comfortably decorated. The red and white striped lighthouse, quaint shops, restaurants, boutique and surrounding picturesque yacht basin are reminiscent of a Mediterranean village.

The villas have easy access to the Harbour Town Golf links and the bustling marina.

One of the most popular resorts in America, we may surmise the 3 championship golf courses add to the over-all attraction.

The Ocean, Sea Marsh, and famed Harbour Town Links are musts on your list for a golfing pleasure. Pete Dye and Jack Nicklaus collaborated on the Harbour Town Links. One of the most famed, innovative courses, it is the site of the familiar Heritage Golf Classic each spring. Challenging and fun for every skill level, the golf courses share one common hazard—natural beauty. Egrets, deer and even an alligator can be seen and even enjoyed.

The island climate is suitable for year round play with a fine staff of Class A PGA teaching professionals. Harbour Town Golf Links 18-hole championship course is rated 74.0 and is 6,652 yards from the championship tees. Small, fast greens, water and sand hazards add to the demand of this course. Sea Marsh, rated 70.0, 18 holes par 72, is 6,372 yards, designed by George Cobb. Ocean Course, rated 71, is 6,600 yards, moderately wide fairways and has an abundance of water, including views of the Atlantic; it was designed by George Cobb.

Besides golf, beaching and enjoying, other sports options are beachcombing, bathing, jogging, deep sea fishing and loads of tennis—truly a golf mecca and an island not to be missed.

*The Inn is a living testimony
to a bygone way of life.*

A new look along with a new name is updating the South's most historic hotel. The new name is "Sheraton," Savannah Inn & Country Club. The world famous Sheraton chain has acquired one of the world's most elegant old hotels, and the combination is dynamic.

The Inn is a refreshing return to an exciting period in our nation's history. You will see reminders of the country's beginnings wherever you turn. For more than a century, the Savannah Inn has been welcoming guests making it the oldest hotel in Georgia. In celebration of the resort's golden anniversary, it has been redecorated in a new "wardrobe."

The guest rooms were all decked out in Southern elegance, and the one we chose even had a four-poster bed. They have not forgotten any of the amenities we expect, I can assure you. The Inn and Country Club combine a sense of "Gone with the Wind" romantic beauty with the recreational facilities of a major new hotel.

When you are a guest, you have full country club privileges. We found the golf course to be interesting, not extremely tough, but enough trouble to keep you alert at all times. We were there during the spring when the lavish azaleas were in bloom and vying for our attention.

When it comes time to dine, the Emerald Room recaptures an era of opulence, and when you taste the exotic food, you will agree that your palate has been rewarded by a master of cookery. When travelling, sometimes the most minute culinary surprise can take on an added importance, and since I am a fiend for the unusual, I especially appreciated the admirably mellow chocolate cup filled with a cream liqueur after dinner.

If dining on the water suits your fancy, Oliver's is for you. It's a sensational nightclub where you will get some of the most succulent steaks, prime rib, and fresh seafood you've ever tasted, served by stylishly dressed "belles." The unique Governor's Lounge, for cocktails, is decorated in fine antiques and paintings to intrigue you.

The spirited boat of "Captain Steve" can take you right from the Inn's marina to downtown Savannah, with cocktails offered to ease your journey. What a treat to see how they have preserved the old wharf; your only problem will be in trying to tear yourself away to journey home.

A magnificent Olympic-size pool with its lovely cabanas deserves applause. With the river as a backdrop, the scene evokes a calm, tranquil mood. There is plenty of deep sea fishing, along with boating and convenient stables for those who want to try different sports.

Everything about the Inn reflects the pages of history and is living testimony to a bygone way of life.

Sheraton Savannah Inn & Country Club
SAVANNAH, GEORGIA

"The South's most historic hotel"

Shipyard plantation is truly one of the most sports-oriented properties of the Hilton Head Company. Accommodations consist of beautiful villas. Rather you choose the Evian or The Cottages you can't miss. The Cottages incorporate the elements of traditional southern charm and comfort. The Evian has elegant French manor style villas situated among fairways and lagoons within the plantation.

Reflections on the green is great for casual dining, and of course the bar is handy.

Shipyard's Racquet club has 24 courts (18 clay and 6 deco). It has been voted by Tennis Magazine as one of the top 50 in the nation.

Of course you can enjoy all the goodies at the beach—bicycling, jogging, etc. Everything you could possibly want out of a golfing vacation is here.

Brigantine is a par 36 3,352 yds., Galleon 3, 364 yds., Clipper 3,466 yds.

Each offers the golfer a challenge or two as he moves across the manicured fairways, among the pines and moss-draped oak trees, around peaceful lagoons and silent ponds. Shipyard is known also for its superior instructional program headed by Ron Cerrudo, who was a member of the U.S. Walker Cup and World Cup teams. At Shipyard, the staff will arrange lessons to suit the needs of any level of golfing expertise. You will enjoy using yours.

Shipyard Plantation

HILTON HEAD ISLAND, SOUTH CAROLINA

If it is golf, good times, peace and quiet, this resort can be the ultimate—and for a variety in golf you can play at Port Royal Plantation, Sea Pines and Palmetto Dunes Plantations also.

The Tides Inn

IRVINGTON, VIRGINIA

For over three decades this resort has been rated by the experts as a Mobil 4-Star and AAA 4-Diamond resort. A quietly beautiful place with only 110 rooms, the Tides Inn is located in the unspoiled part of Eastern Virginia known as the Northern Neck, a peninsula formed by the Potomac and Rappahannock Rivers. It is protected by remoteness and charmed with history.

Your tastefully appointed accommodations are the epitome of the understated elegance that is their hallmark and most of the rooms face the water. Known for their wonderful food, acclaimed meals are skillfully served in beautiful settings of fine linen, china, silverware and crystal for formal dining. Luncheons and cocktails are served informally poolside, and if a picture speaks 1,000 words you're in for a special treat as the views are spectacular while you dine, with the backdrop of not only the pool but the river backs up to it. An unusual and highly popular luncheon spot is Cap'n B's.

For a casual luncheon and cocktails, poolside at the Summer House is perfect. If you want even more excitement, choose a trip aboard one of the Inn's three yachts or dine in the club at the Golden Eagle. Perhaps the Unique Binnacle Restaurant overlooking the marina.

 This certainly can be a golfer's dream as you choose from 45 great golf holes. The Golden Eagle is a recognized course designed by well-known architect George Cobb. It is an 18-hole championship course but every type of golfer can enjoy it. It measures 6,943 yards.

The Tartan course is another of their 18-hole courses at their sister resort The Tides Lodge. You may play it as a guest of the hotel. And as though this were not enough, you have the 9-hole course for sharpening up your short game.

Their lovely Pro shop can be a pleasant place to shop, incidentally, it is just a short 200 yards away and you can boat ride across the river on the Gondola or van services are available to take you a short distance to the golf courses.

Swimming, boating, yachting and plenty of tennis are only part of the options awaiting your pleasant stay. If it's peace, beauty and serenity you are looking for, you will be a welcomed guest, as they love to "pamper."

"A golfer's paradise:

The Tides Lodge

IRVINGTON, VIRGINIA

Emphasizing luxury in an informal setting One of America's most authentic Scottish Lodges.

THE TIDES LODGE

Irvington, Virginia

The Tides Lodge is a small resort emphasizing luxury in an informal setting, on their own peninsula a few miles from Chesapeake Bay, the commanding views are spectacular. Being one of America's most authentic Scottish Lodges, it is located in rural Virginia.

Known for super service with better than one staff member for each guest assures you unparalleled attention. Luxurious accommodations range from Select, Deluxe, Semi-suites or Suites. Attractively decorated they are graced with all the amenities of a gracious home.

For your appetite the Lodge features the Royal Stewart Dining Room where the food is highly praised for its innovative cuisine. After 6:00 p.m. gentlemen must wear a coat.

The Binnacle promises the best seafood in Virginia and you should thoroughly enjoy the panoramic view. Always a fun spot poolside is where you can create your own favorite sandwich while enjoying the resort atmosphere. After dinner you may want to take a moonlight cruise on one of their private yachts, or dance until dawn.

In 1959 the resident architect of the Royal and Ancient in St. Andrews, Scotland, Sir Guy Campbell, spent the season at the Lodge where he designed his first American Golf Course. With his deep respect and love for the game, you know the nine holes he completed before his death had to be very special.

The eminent George Cobb designed the other nine holes in superb style and now this course is very well played and in demand. The Tartan golf course is just a short distance from your room. It is a par 72 and it is an 18-hole championship course.

Of course, the unique thing about the Tides Lodge is the fact that it is a golfing haven, with the Tides Inn just across the bay, boats shuttle you with good service.

There you can't miss playing the Tides Inn Golden Eagle Course or opting for the nine hole executive course to improve your short game.

I recommend this as one of America's most unique and charming resorts. Besides boating you have panorama salt water and heated fresh water pools, tennis, shuffleboard and all marine activities. Rowboats, canoes, sailboats are available and no charge to their guests.

Turnberry Isle Yacht and Country Club

MIAMI, FLORIDA

Rapidly becoming a land of legends, Turnberry sits on over 300 acres of breathtaking tropical gardens, pools, and waterways. Playing here is a magical refuge from la vie ordinaire, sparkling day and night with the stars of stage, screen, sports, finance and the arts.

Located along the Intracoastal Waterway, it is the home and playground of some of the most celebrated people. Curving softly around the entrance of the yacht harbor, the Marina hotel is the quintessence of a small, private European hotel. The 120 rooms are extraordinary with impeccable appointments. Fine woods, fabrics and tiles, jacuzzi baths and sweeping terraces, to mention a few. Across the tropical fairways at the Country Club Inn deluxe suites 1600 square feet, include a double Jacuzzi, private rooftop solarium and redwood hot tub. Both are whisper-quiet with an international staff.

Two spectacular golf courses await your playing pleasure. Sitting among 243 acres, they are breathtakingly beautiful. Under the capable direction of pro Julius Boros, who personally oversees the meticulously kept greens and lush fairways. Home of the PGA Senior's Tournaments, the Turnberry South Course is 6,899 yards of fun, challenge, and excitement. The North Course measures 6,327 yards and is a typical South Florida course designed by Robert Trent Jones. If you can deal with a lot of water and sand, you will like it here.

It has been the home of the Elizabeth Arden LPGA tournament and many others because of the desireability. More than a club—it is another world, *touting the world's largest triple green on hole #2 on the south course.*

"refuge from la vie ordinaire"

If you are looking for a beautiful place for R & R, you can unwind here among the style in terrace lounges and restaurants, reflecting pools, fountains and a terrific staff. Complete with an internationally recognized spa, there is a doctor for your physicals and a staff of professionals to gear your personal fitness program, including diet and nutrition.

Tennis is an integral part of this famed resort and it also plays host to the Pro-Celebrity Tennis Classic. 24 courts with 18 lit for night play.

Aside from all this there is more—the World Championship Backgammon is held here.

The Ocean Club, located directly on the wave-swept beach of the Atlantic Ocean, is a busy place. Truly a World Class Resort, your dining experiences are extraordinarily diversified. The Monaco Dining Room is a marvelously scenic, three-tiered restaurant featuring haute cuisine prepared by internationally award-winning chefs.

For more casual fare, poolside dining in the Sunset Cafe at the Marine Hotel can be just the ticket, or for a romantic evening you may opt for a gourmet cruise. A 13,000 square foot facility caters to a business conference and its unique surroundings make it a superb choice.

The World of Palm-Aire

POMPANO BEACH, FLORIDA

Luxurious and distinctive accommodations are characteristic of this fine resort.

Just one of four beautifully appointed restaurants serving guests at The World of Palm-Aire.

The World of Palm-Aire is a beautiful modern resort located at Pompano Beach, Florida. Dedicated to the health and fitness of its guests, the resort is famous for its elaborate spa and fitness programs, but its five golf courses are an attraction for me.

Luxurious in every respect, the 1,500-acre Palm-Aire caters to the outdoor-oriented guest. In addition to the golf courses, there are 37 night-lighted tennis courts, swimming pools, a beach club, racquetball courts, and a par course with exercise stations for the runners.

Guests at Palm-Aire can select from four beautifully-appointed restaurants. Those on the fitness program have their own dining room, the Spa Dining Room, which serves delicious calorie-controlled meals. For the rest of us, there's a choice of some of the finest food in Florida. For example, the menu at the beautiful Peninsula Room lists such specialties as local seafood, milk-fed veal, and fresh green salads.

Evenings feature entertainment and dancing in one of the resort's lovely cocktail lounges. And by day many guests enjoy cool drinks served poolside.

Accommodations at Palm-Aire are luxurious. Rooms are spacious, sunny, richly appointed. Each has a private dressing room and a terrace.

Imagine five golf courses! You'd never have a chance to get bored even if all you did was play golf. There are four 18-hole championship courses and one nine-hole executive course; each offers a different challenge. And because there are so many options, the golfer never has to wait for a tee-time; you can always get on a course.

It is very peaceful at the Palm-Aire. Nowhere is that more evident than on the golf courses with their expansive fairways. There's little hill-climbing here, but plenty of opportunity to enjoy the beautiful Florida scenery, the tropical trees, and colorful flowers.

The World of Palm-Aire is within 20 minutes of Fort Lauderdale International Airport on Pompano Parkway opposite Pompano Harness Track. This is a place where you can really pamper yourself and enjoy your favorite sport at the same time.

Americana Lake Geneva

LAKE GENEVA, WISCONSIN

Golf Digest has chosen this resort as one of the top "10" in North America.

Since this is a year-round golf and ski resort on 1,400 acres overlooking a private lake, it is a favorite of many world-class travelers. A low-rise, eight-building complex of cedar-textured concrete and glass, it has 340 rooms including 55 suites, all with air conditioning and color TV's. For your convenience, their staff speaks fluent English, German, and French.

A resort with much to do and only 90 minutes from Chicago, the Americana is nestled in a true country setting and boasts something for everybody, especially a golfer.

Your luxurious accommodations are complete with private balcony or patio, and they overlook the lush Wisconsin countryside.

Many dining options are available, depending upon your mood. If you care to be casual, the Sidewalk Cafe will suit you well, or try Annie's, where you can always depend on just the right food. Dining on the more elegant side can be a winner in the Americana Steakhouse with evening entertainment. After dinner, you can relax in the beautiful piano bar and enjoy your favorite night-cap.

Golf enthusiasts can enjoy two 18-hole championship courses, plus the driving range. The beautiful Brute is demanding but can certainly offer a "unique" encounter. Many golfers consider this course one of the best they have ever played. This Par 72, designed by Robert Bruce Harris, measures 7,258 yards and features over 70 bunkers, numerous water hazards, rolling hills, and an abundance of trees. The greens are supposed to be among the largest in the world, averaging over 10,000 square feet each.

You can count on the "Brute" being a brute.

The Briar Patch, a Par 71, designed by Peter Dye and Jack Nicklaus, measures 6,900 yards and is quite different from the Brute, having little water, few trees, and small greens. Dotted with heather and high natural rough, the Briar Patch could pass as a sister of the Scottish-style courses.

If you enjoy a touch of Scotland, this course can certainly transport you back, while providing a test of golf that requires precision and exacting shots.

After golf you can shop in a great pro shop that offers a variety of equipment and golf clothing.

Americana Lake Geneva Resort is a popular conference center. Whatever your recreation desires, there's plenty of it here, including heated indoor and outdoor pools, indoor sports complex for tennis, a Nautilus fitness center, men's and women's health spa, horseback riding, sailing on their private lake, skeet and trap shooting plus miniature golf and much, much more.

Year-round golf and ski resort only 90 minutes from Chicago.

Eagle Ridge Inn & Resort

GALENA, ILLINOIS

*One of the most
exciting courses in
the midwest today.*

The Galena Territory

In the Northwest corner of Illinois, perched on a ridge overlooking Lake Galena, this 66-room inn is a blend of an old New England inn with all the modern conveniences you would find at a vacation retreat. The rooms are spacious, featuring spectacular views of the lake and rolling hills, and are decorated with furnishings reminiscent of the 19th century.

Some suites have wood-burning fireplaces and private jacuzzis. Guests savor American and continenal cuisine in an atmosphere of warmth and friendliness. From the moment you enter the dining room, the view of Lake Galena is ever-present with her commanding view. Menus in the adjacent breakfast and luncheon room offer delightful selections with an equally spectacular view.

A confirmation about the food—Mobil Travel Guide has given a Three Star rating for the fourth year in a row, recognizing it as one in the top 2% of all hotels and resorts of North America.

The Inn's Springhouse Tap features live entertainment, and it is a gathering spot for before or after dinner drinks.

Sporting not only one, but two, golf courses, both were designed by Roger Packard. Both courses combine the territory's unique terrain with a challenging and scenic layout. In 1983, the north course was named by the American Society of Golf Course Architects as one of the top 25 new golf courses in the country. The south course, which opened the summer of 1984, was chosen by Golf Digest as one of the "Best New Resort Courses" for 1984.

The Eagle Ridge south course plays tighter on the fairways than the north course and has much more water. Some hazards are in the form of lakes, ponds, meandering streams, and cascading waterfalls. The south course is 6762 yards, the north course 7012 yards from the championship tees.

Noted for its impressive beauty and challenging terrain, the American Society of Golf Course Architects have selected it as one of the top 25 new courses.

Far from the distractions of a crowded city environment, Eagle Ridge Inn provides the ideal climate for business and social gatherings.

Aside from golf, one of the largest riding centers in the midwest is here with indoor arena, 7,309 square feet. Boating, fishing, ice skating, winter tobogganing, tubing and horse-drawn sleigh rides add a sporting pleasure. In winter it is a cross-country ski resort.

The Inn's magnificent natural setting provides a refreshing atmosphere, complete with a conference center, too. If you are looking for a real change in vacation hideaways with everything and maybe more than you expect, try it—you will like it.

If you are looking for an exotic paradise, as we were when we found the Lodge of the Four Seasons, you are invited to visit this internationally renowned resort community in a carefully preserved environment of natural beauty. Totally surrounded by inlets and coves that shape one of the largest lakes in America, the Lodge has loveliness everywhere you look.

The buildings have been conceived in such a way as to blend perfectly with the environment. Extensive Japanese gardens, along with other plantings and the sparkling, unpolluted waters of the lake, provide "a place like no other." The rustic, but elegantly and colorfully decorated rooms have been aptly named The Treetops and The Water's Edge. Accommodations are done in glass from ceiling to floor and are completely furnished right down to your toaster.

Waterfalls are numerous and lend a mystical charm to this perfect hideaway.

When you tee off on this 18-hole championship course, you will certainly recognize that Robert Trent Jones has been here and created a super layout. All 6,500 yards wind over and under, around and through the Ozark hills, slopes, and plains. You might say that the course resembles Pebble Beach, boasting breathtaking water views, but the comparison is insufficient. This course is truly unique.

An internationally renowned, exotic paradise where you will enjoy the sparkling, unpolluted water of one of the largest lakes in America.

Some of the holes are played right on the brink of the peninsula, fingering into the lake. Of the many courses one plays, here, it seems your shot cannot be articulate enough.

You may be pleasantly distracted if you start enjoying the scenery too much, and your score may not be as good as you would like. But with the variety of holes awaiting you in the overall panorama, this could be but a small problem.

As you cross lakes and inlets, you can appreciate their 3 Pars as some of the most interesting and challenging you have ever played.

Now you're ready for some good news: FOOD — delightful payment after a hard day. Chef Torres, who previously served the King of Morocco, is responsible for the French food in the Toledo Supper Club, where you will eat imaginative cuisine in this quiet heartland setting. To add to a perfect evening, you will be serenaded by their violinist and guitarist.

On the lighter side, you may enjoy an *aperitif* in Ted's Place, where a marvelous job has been done to create an old English pub. The stained glass windows are certain to catch your eye, along with brass rails and beamed ceilings. Another special treat is the wonderful music of their harpist.

Serving on the casual side, H.K.'s sizzles turkey steaks on an open-view grill — and they are something else! If calories are not worth counting, I predict you'll spend some time in the Pastry Shop. A most popular spot, serving incomparable Hunters-Style Brunch, is the Country Deli.

From Stetsons and cowboy boots in the Wild Time Saloon to romantic evenings in silks, the variety of this versatile resort will bring you back time and again, as it has for so many traveling golfers.

For a healthy stay, you will want to check out the spa, maybe do some swimming, or play a little tennis.

Mother Nature has been busy creating a blaze of color and excitement for you here, and the Lodge blends these natural wonders with harmonious cordiality by a staff of international influence to serve you with terrific flavor.

Lodge of the Four Seasons

LAKE OZARK, MISSOURI

"Coves, inlets, waterfalls add mystical charm"

Marriott's Tan-Tar-A

OSAGE BEACH, MISSOURI

"1,500 miles of shoreline"

Marriott's Tan-Tar-A is a special resort. It's a favorite because of its beautiful setting on a peninsula in lovely Lake of the Ozarks, Missouri. The lake itself, with its 1,500 miles of shoreline, splendid beaches, and water recreation is worth a visit. But staying at Tan-Tar-A gives the visit an extraordinary quality.

The hotel, which is about 20 years old, has recently been renovated and it shows in the beautifully decorated guest rooms, the elegant and comfortable restaurants, and the splendid grounds.

The hotel has five excellent restaurants, each offering a bit of a different experience. Perhaps the most unusual is the Happy House which is virtually carved from the side of the hill. The Alpine Haus exudes a Bavarian charm; it is popular for its extensive menu of steaks, fowl, and game. The Cliff Room also sports a Bavarian theme, but it is an elegant room featuring superb gourmet cuisine. On Sundays, the Cliff Room becomes a brunch paradise as the Marriot chefs present their famous, stupendous buffet; the brunch at Tan-Tar-A is unusually bountiful and beautiful with flowers and ice sculptures everywhere. Finally, the Windrose is a popular dining spot with those who visit the marina in summer. Dancing and good entertainment are to be found at the Der Krug Lounge.

Tan-Tar-A has 800 romantic guest rooms and suites. The rooms are beautifully decorated in a style which suits the resort's Ozark setting. Early American and Indian artifacts are extensively used. Many of the rooms have private flower-decked patios or balconies with views of the lake.

Elegant gourmet cuisine with a Bavarian theme. Dining here is a memorable experience.

Twenty-seven beautiful holes of golf await the golfer. The Oaks is a 6,328-yard, 18-hole challenge. Accuracy is the key on this relatively short course where the obstacles are tight fairways bounded by heavy foliage, hilly terrain, ponds, waterholes, and small greens. Ninety-seven sandtraps can be disgusting.

A smaller nine-hole executive course offers many of the same challenges.

But the lure here is the view. At every turn, it seems, your eyes will behold a view of the lake. Perhaps you will feel its effect on your game when you add up your scorecard and discover that you failed to keep your eye on the ball.

Capitalizing on beauty, service, and integrity, Tan-Tar-A has become one of the most popular vacation resorts in the Midwest.

Indoor racquetball and two tennis courts, plus a complete health club and an indoor ice skating rink are available for your pleasure, along with horseback riding and trap shooting. Or you may just choose to relax and sunbask on a sandy beach.

Marriott

Olympia Resort and Spa

OCONOMOWOC, WISCONSIN

Surrounding this luxury resort is a dramatic, natural setting of forest, hills, rivers, and lakes.

Created by a famous team of architects and designers, this exclusive resort/sports/convention complex is the ultimate in design and decor, and an ambitious undertaking in the Midwest.

Blending with a dramatic natural setting of forest, hills, rivers, and lakes, this complete luxury resort of stunning modern structure lies in the southern Wisconsin lake country and offers a myriad of sports and facilities. We were impressed with its magnitude.

The outdoor beauty is just the beginning. Once inside, your

warm greeting begins with a fireplace wall sweeping to the sky, celestial windows, massive skylights, and handsomely beamed ceilings. Arriving at this friendly and casual (but sophisticated) resort automatically lifts your spirit.

Five hundred rooms and villas—luxury accommodations—offer outstanding views of the golf course, pool, lake, or ski hill. Enjoying spacious and plush, colorfully decorated rooms, all with private bar and open fireplace, you will live in ultimate comfort.

Challenging your golfing skills are lush fairways, bordered by lakes and streams. Teeing off on this beautifully maintained course (that's a gem in design, measuring 6,600 yards) requires thought and accuracy. The profusion of lateral and parallel water hazards requires serious concentration, and a number of criss-cross holes among the small lakes and streams also come into play.

After your workout on the links, your mood will undoubtedly steer toward a relaxing evening. A variety of superb dining opportunities awaits you from gourmet to an informal atmosphere, all sure to enhance your evening's "bill of fare." The Terrace is the main dining room decorated attractively and comfortably for your enjoyment. European and American dishes are prepared with flair and served at a leisurely pace.

The Beach House at lovely Silver Lake is the charming and informal place to dine—a winner every time. You will feast heartily on fresh seafood, steaks, and chops. The Hotel Coffee Shop is open for lunch, snacks, and casual dining. The Clubhouse is the light-hearted setting for happy hour and high spirits. This is truly a place where as the sun goes down, the spirit perks up.

After dinner, top performers and musical groups provide great entertainment, or you may wish to view movies at one of the Twin Cinemas.

For a new adventure—and a million dollar figure and improved health—have fun while slimming down in separate health clubs for men and women (whirlpool, sauna, steam baths, Grecian showers, and sun lamps). An experienced staff of trained spa personnel will assist you.

Now you know where to start if you want to bring your body back to life and emerge with a sense of exhilaration—Olympia Resort and Spa—where fun, friendly people, your favorite sports, perfect dining, and night life contribute to your sense of a pampered holiday.

"A dramatic and ambitious undertaking"

The Admiralty Resort

PORT LUDLOW, WASHINGTON

Provides immediate access to the deep blue waters of Puget Sound.

With the Olympic Mountains as a backdrop and located on Washington's Puget Sound, Port Ludlow's Admiralty Resort is a haven for sportsmen. In the quiet pleasures of the Olympic National Forest, you can find perfect relaxation. Only about 25 miles from Seattle, you will have access to an emerald-colored water wonderland. The deep pines and cedar forests create a setting for splendid solitude.

As you check into one of The Admiralty Resort's private units, you may select from deluxe bedroom and bath combinations to spacious suites with a living room, kitchen, fireplace, and private deck. You may also have a one- or four-bedroom suite. You will love the award winning architecture, as we did; it blends so harmoniously with the surroundings.

We found dining to be excellent. The Harbormaster Restaurant will please you with a wide offering of the most tasty foods. If you're looking for more laid-back relaxation, try their intimate lounge. The drinks, food, and service are number one.

The golf course has had so many honors bestowed upon it lately, it's hard to remember them all, but one thing is for certain: when they were honored for being the Northwest's best course, it was obvious why.

Describing The Admiralty as the Northwest's most beautiful course as well could be hearsay. You'll just have to check it out and decide for yourself.

Another honor was having one of the prettiest holes, a Par 3 #17. It deserved this award. The course was also voted one of the most enjoyable to play. U.S. *Golf Digest* has placed this course among the "top three dozen public courses."

From the blue tees, it plays 6,787 yards and is a Par 73. You will find the course always in impeccable condition and fun to play amid the natural beauty. Designed by Peter Muir Graves, it is one course that is as challenging as it is scenic. Distance is important, but accuracy is a must.

Strolling, hiking, beachcombing, and bicycling are popular sports and pastimes, as are clamming and crabbing, and you can do it here in clear, clean water. Their modern 300-slip saltwater marina provides immediate access to deep blue waters of Puget Sound.

You can arrive conveniently by amphibious aircraft right to the Admiralty's front lawn. If you're coming from Seattle, by prior arrangement they will be delighted to pick you up.

With all the honors bestowed upon this great resort, their greatest will be having you as their guest.

"In the quiet pleasures of the forest, perfect relaxation"

Each year since 1960, this Grand Resort Hotel has received a Mobil Five-Star Rating, to earn the reputation as an elder statesman of grand resort hotels. It was no surprise to me.

Reminiscent of the finest European tradition, the Broadmoor is a blend of old world grace and charm and of modern convenience. For years, their uncompromising dedication to quality and service has drawn thousands of visitors (including me).

I remember being very excited by what I was seeing upon my first visit: handworked details, exquisite art and architecture, and elaborate appointments. To repeat a cliche, Broadmoor is a city in itself; friendly and without traffic, smog or revolving doors.

Since 1918, the Broadmoor Main has been extending a warm welcome. It houses three famous dining rooms: the Tavern which is bright and informal, the tropical Garden Room, and the stately Main Dining Room.

Broadmoor South presents the world-famous Penrose Room, named after Spencer Penrose who was the originator of the hotel. This restaurant is an accurate reflection of the Edwardian era, with a European flavor. It features city and mountain views, a live orchestra at lunch and dinner, and a varied menu.

Broadmoor West presents outstanding dining and authentic English country house manor decor.

Spec's Spot offers nightclub entertainment in an atmosphere reminiscent of the twenties.

The BROADMOOR

Few golf complexes in the world compare with the championship credentials of the 54 holes you have to choose from here. It was hard for me to concentrate while admiring the outstanding grandeur of the Rocky Mountain backdrop. The East Course was designed by Donald Ross and is 7,218 yards, Par 72; the 6,937-yard, Par 72 West Course is a Robert Trent Jones; and the South Course, also Par 72 and 6,935 yards, was designed by the Arnold Palmer Organization. What a representation!

There is something here for every golfer, regardless of your handicap.

Located 15 minutes from downtown Colorado Springs, Broadmoor is easily accessible by nation-wide direct jet service.

In nature and in the works of man, perfection in livable human proportion is both alluring and elusive. Happily, we found it in residence at the Broadmoor.

Recreational facilities are varied and include tennis, skiing, ice skating, horseback riding, and bicycling.

I recommend clothing matches for the climate and the lifestyle. For the nights, you'll need some medium-weight items. Daytime dress is casual, but after 6:00 p.m. gentlemen are requested to wear coats and ties.

The Broadmoor

COLORADO SPRINGS, COLORADO

Best thing about golfing at The Broadmoor is your tee time availability with so many courses to choose from. Left, 18th hole of the Robert Trent Jones-designed West Course; below, view of the Main and South Hotels from across the lake.

Keystone

KEYSTONE, COLORADO

Five Diamond Award from the American Automobile Association, and a Four Star rating from Mobile Travel Guide.

Keystone is a complete resort village holding the prestigious Five Diamond award from the American Automobile Association, and a Four Star rating from the Mobile Travel Guide for superiority of guest facilities, service and atmosphere. Offering spectacular mountain views from each of its 152 rooms, most with private balconies. All rooms are tastefully and comfortably decorated, some feature a sitting room and loft bedroom.

Private homes as well as condominiums are also available throughout the Keystone Village and Resort. Luxuriously appointed, they are spacious and offer the ultimate in vacation living. A swimming pool, sauna or jacuzzi is available at most condominium locations.

Accommodating every appetite and every budget, your options for restaurants go from the Elegant Garden Room for continental dining and Sunday Brunch to the Bighorn Steakhouse for succulent steaks and prime rib.

If you enjoy a western setting, the Keystone Ranch Golf Course offers dining in a restored 50-year old ranchhouse with its elegant living room, dining room and bar where service matches the decor.

Golf at Keystone is the "ultimate," a Robert Trent Jones, Jr. design. It is a championship golf course, overlooking the Rocky Mountain Valley. Reminiscent of the legendary courses of Scotland and England, it is a masterpiece. It has been said he sculpted the woodlands and meadows into a challenging work of art.

The 18-hole 7,090-yard course retains the flavor of the area, first settled in 1870. The nine-acre lake is a special feature and playing across is simply a challenge, but adds a zing of excitement. The trees, links and water, plus the overview of the valley add to the Old West ambience.

Other activities available are John Gardiner's Tennis ranch featuring 14 championship courts, two of which are indoors.

Rafting is famous at this resort. Horseback riding, hayrides, sailing on spectacular Lake Dillon. Swimming, western barbeques and jeep tours add to the all-over sporting options. Boating on Keystone Lake, hiking and backpacking, plus fishing are available.

"A natural phenomenon tucked in the Oregon forest"

Salishan Lodge

GLENEDIN BEACH, OREGON

The spectacular Oregon Coast beckons one and all. Fresh clear air plus majestic backdrops produce an atmosphere conducive to total enjoyment at the Salishan Lodge (Five-Star rated, plus the Triple AAA Five Diamond Award).

Comparatively simple wood has been used sumptuously, making a most beautiful modern hotel. The whole complex of buildings looks like a natural phenomenon tucked in the Oregon forest near the sea.

Producing every possible touch of comfort, 150 distinctively styled guest rooms, each with a fireplace and view balcony, are scattered around the main lodge.

If you enjoy variety, may I introduce you to their Gourmet Room with abundant seafood delicacies and haute cuisine from around the world served in a gracious atmosphere. Be prepared for a gourmet's extravaganza.

The cheery Sun Room and Coffee Shop has superior selections from snacks to dinners — mmmmmm so good! And the Cedar Tree is alive with music to set you dancing, yet romantic enough for your candlelight dinners. They are famous for potlatch salmon barbeques and savory steaks charcoaled over Mexican mesquite — always a favorite. The Attic Lounge lends a real coziness with the large stone fireplace being one of the main attractions.

Salishan now has a 920-bin wine cellar housing 40,000 bottles of 1,000 different choices. In 1982 *Wine Spectator* honored them as one of the top 100 restaurant wine lists in the United States. The cellar is next to the Gourmet Restaurant and is open to the public.

Travel Holiday Magazine has honored Salishan with their Fine Dining Award since 1972, assuring that you are in good hands.

Salishan and golf go together perfectly. Keeping in the Scottish tradition of oceanside golfing, the 18-hole course is as beautiful as the coast it bounds. If you talk with well traveled golfers, rest assured that if Oregon is mentioned, Salishan will be the favorite. The Par 72 is as enjoyable as it is beautiful, but the tall pines can get you into trouble unless you keep your eye on the ball. Needless to say, water holes, dog-legs, and bunkers will be lurking here and there.

Aside from all this, if you carry a tennis racquet for extra sporting pleasures, indoor and outdoor courts provide modern performance-proven surfaces.

Hiking trails cover 750 acres of forest preserve where you can see one of the world's most magnificent collections of driftwood on three miles of secluded beach on the Salishan Peninsula. Deep-sea fishing is just minutes away. Swim in the huge indoor pool; swirl in the hydro-therapy pool; or enjoy a sauna.

Salishan proudly boasts a great collection of paintings from Northwest artists. If you are ready for new discoveries, Salishan is your answer.

Sun Valley Lodge

SUN VALLEY, IDAHO

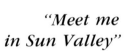

"Meet me in Sun Valley"

Today Sun Valley is just as romantic as it ever was. This winter-ski-resort / summer-golf-resort has recently been refurbished to bring it up to the standards we expect. But the refurbishment has not altered the charm of this mountain hideaway one bit; it's only made it more attractive and more comfortable.

Rooms are attractive, meticulously appointed to appeal to the most particular guest. They're colorfully decorated with an intimate, romantic atmosphere.

Guests who stay for any length of time in Sun Valley will want to try all of the resort's fine restaurants. Each offers fine food and fabulous drinks.

The Lodge Dining Room is known for its elegant cuisine and wonderful Sunday brunches. The Ore House features those scrumptious Idaho steaks as well as Maine lobster. Steaks are also the specialty at the Ram Restaurant which prides itself on cooking them exactly as you want them . . . rare, medium or well. Those who enjoy Italian food will definitely want to try the cuisine at Penguini's where spaghetti and pizza grace the menu. And for those on the go — and you will be one of them in Sun Valley — the Continental Cafeteria offers quick, easy service.

For those romantic evenings we mentioned, there's dancing to the soft music in the Duchin Bar and Lounge.

 Like the hotel, the golf course has recently been rebuilt. In 1979–80, Robert Trent Jones redesigned the 18-hole course into a Par 71 tough championship challenge, and has dubbed his course a masterpiece. There are elevated tees, tree-lined fairways, luscious greens guarded by many sand traps and sparkling Trail Creek. This course has one other distraction not found everywhere — its wildlife wandering nearby. Scenery is beautiful of course with the ragged Sawtooth Mountains serving as a backdrop. Here's wishing you a beautiful game to match.

Sun Valley is much more than a hotel. Everything you could need is available in the nearby town. And there is a variety of recreational activities to select from: bicycling, horseback riding, swimming, tennis, volleyball, archery, and ice skating on the world-renowned rink.

Recapture the romance of the past with the comfort and convenience of the present at this famous resort!

Sun Valley reaches out and takes your heart. The movie magic of the Forties lingers on.

The sun almost never forgets to shine here, where 263 days a year I'm told that it holds a captive audience. Sunriver is a multi-million-dollar magnificent resort situated on several thousand well-developed Oregon acres 15 miles south of Bend. It left a mark on our minds and on our spirits, long after we left its spectacular sunrises and sunsets behind.

"The fun never sets at Sunriver"

I remember two championship golf courses to choose from, making it a perfect start to each day as we wondered "Shall it be the North Course, designed by Robert Trent Jones II, or the South Course?" Keep in mind, the North Course is a little shorter.

Literally carved out of the native central Oregon land to provide a tranquil setting, it is truly a top-notch northeast course by my standards. Golfers of any calibre will find a terrific challenge.

The site of the Sunriver Oregon Open in 1982, it has the honor of being named for 1983 and 1984 Opens as well.

We found these courses to be far from the ordinary golf course because of the meticulous care they receive and the beauty of the surroundings. Playing them was a most memorable and enjoyable experience. Nearly every hole plays as a dog leg. The course has more than 50 greenside traps; seven were very large and always in play. Considering the lakes and the pines, a golfer must display accuracy.

Sunriver

BEND, OREGON

The accommodations are superior. In addition to the 360 condominium hotel rooms, there are 77 deluxe and spacious bedroom units with deluxe kitchen suites available. All are operated by the Lodge and nestled along the links or next to the national forest. The tasteful interiors will make it hard for you to select whether you want a loft bedroom, dining room, large living room, or just a bedroom. Take your pick, they're all available.

Sunrise Lodge houses a beautiful main dining room, Potter's Wheel Restaurant, Steak Deck, and an Owl's Nest Lounge. You will find the atmosphere in the Potter's Wheel Restaurant to be friendly and relaxed. The Meadows is for wining and dining, enjoying some carefully prepared continental cuisine. The wine list is superb. We found it to be a most convivial place to please our palates; I think you will, too.

When the central Oregon stars put on their evening performance, and you're in the mood, you can enjoy some musical stars performing in the Owl's Nest seven nights a week.

Whatever your pleasure, Sunriver has it. Racquetball, swimming, bicycling, horseback riding, canoeing, or fishing — or just plain relaxing — are available in the fresh clean air, blue skies, and peaceful surroundings. They say the "fun" never sets at Sunriver.

Tamarron

DURANGO, COLORADO

*"Beauty
that radiates
quality"*

Adventurously inspired by the local mountains, lakes, and streams, the Tamarron Hotel and Resort presents an incomparable setting, with views that command your attention. A year-round resort, Tamarron has received the prestigious American Automobile Association's Five Diamond award and Mobil's Four Star Award.

Accommodations include 312 beautifully furnished condominium units. As particular as I am, I can honestly say that the suites added an extra dimension to our visit. The aura of beauty surrounding us radiated quality.

At this writing, 99 more condominiums at Highpoint are under construction. All rooms are spaciously designed and furnished to carry through the resort's motif of rustic elegance. Large rooms for two, for four, and for six are available with private balconies and fireplaces.

 Visually stunning views from the 18-hole championship golf course are worth the trip. Each hole has been designed to blend with the finest scenery in Colorado.

This course has been meticulously groomed for champions. Though no easy course (it is challenging for the best golfer), amateurs love it because of its spectacular beauty and interesting set-up. From the moment you tee off, you will know that you must play to the best of your ability.

The resort staff has the perfect knack for knowing what to do for their guests in the dining room. The service is impeccable and will please the most discriminating diner.

The gifted chef prepares culinary delights fit for royalty; and here, you are royalty. His insistence on fresh produce, exquisite flavor, and rich bouquet combined with the style in which it is served turns your meal into an uncommon pleasure. Additional touches of live dinner music and fresh flowers, add to your occasion. I love the waiters' white gloves, too. How long has it been since you've seen this? ? ?

The San Juan Club is a family-style restaurant which is open through the day or for a late-night snack. Upbeat entertainment is presented nightly. The rustic Mineshaft Lounge is a casual entertainment center which offers movies at night. Overlooking Le Canyon on the second level is the Windom Peak Lounge featuring live entertainment.

An integral part of Tamarron's make-up is the endless list of activities. Some of these are tennis, a fully-staffed health club, pools, and spa. Emphasis is put on horseback riding and bicycling.

An exciting sidetrip we made was to Silverton on a narrow gauge train. It takes three hours. And what pleasant hours they are, since you travel through the unspoiled terrain. Silverton is a very quaint and authentic mining town. We ate at a place called the "Bent Elbow Saloon" and I really felt like a part of the old gold rush days. The train has been running for 80 years, and I'm sure that the saloon's pianist rode on the original train trip. You will love her and her no-nonsense approach. Buy her a drink for me...thanks.

Located 18 miles north of Durango, Colorado, and eight miles south of Purgatory, Tamarron is easily accessible. If you are planning a business convention, they have facilities for up to 600 people.

"A Shangri-la of rustic excellence and luxury"

Alisal

SOLVANG, CALIFORNIA

Sense of being alone with nature in unmatched serenity, framed and studded with oak trees, lures the traveling golfer time and time again.

When you enter the gates of the Alisal Ranch, it's as though you're taking a trip into the past. Within the 10,000 acres surrounded by sycamores and oaks, you will discover a Shangri-la of rustic elegance and luxury.

Enthusiastic western-clad desk clerks at the registration desk set the stage for what is about to become your western adventure.

The majority of the staff has been with the ranch for years so they know just how to treat you. It works. Their guests return repeatedly.

I remember so well, during our last visit, as we were driving to our rustic but elegant cottage, a beautiful little fawn raised its head from some lush greenery as if to say "welcome." Hundreds of wild deer graze the Alisal and it is not uncommon for them to come right down along the golf course.

The 18-hole golf course is as beautiful as it is challenging. I can attest to the fact you can hardly ever find the same lie. Water comes into play on several holes, but the thing we noticed most were the pervasive traps that were always in our way.

The course is framed and studded with ancient oaks and sycamores. It is a William Bell design 6,354 yards long, but it seems to play much longer. The thing we enjoyed best is that every detail is so impeccably tended. Trees and shrubs are pruned to perfection. Flowering plants are placed to add a touch of bright color everywhere.

The importance the ranch places on the food and service is reflected in every touch. Dining tables were set as if each was a theatre ready for a nightly performance. We found the food to rate an encore.

You may enjoy the Oak Room, a rustic lounge, where the focal point is an enormous fireplace which adds to the already-warm friendliness. The poolside bar is always busy and it's nearly always pool weather here.

Aside from golf, they have tennis facilities, horseback riding, swimming, bubbling hot water spas, and boating on their own 90-acre lake. A recreation room is available for informal dancing, square dancing and western entertainment. For quieter moments, there is a library for reading, watching TV and card-playing.

Accommodations range from studios, to two-room suites, two-room loft suites, or private bungalows "on the lake." These bungalows have a large front porch, three bedrooms, two baths and a large front room. Of course, each has its own fireplace and pleasant decor.

Alisal has enjoyed many years of success, and it is for this reason that reservations are essential. Be aware that this is a family-owned working ranch, so be ready for a touch of "the real west." If you are arriving from Los Angeles, take San Marcos Pass Road just outside Santa Barbara to Solvang, turn left on Alisal Road. If you are leaving from San Francisco, take U.S. 101 south, turn left at Buellton and go three miles to Solvang; turn right on Alisal Road. From here, it's three miles to Alisal's main gate.

The weather is sunny for more than 300 days each year and winters are crisp, but clear. Casual clothes are fine for the day, but gentlemen must wear jackets at dinner.

The Arizona Biltmore

PHOENIX, ARIZONA

A half-century of tradition awaits those who will visit the Arizona Biltmore, completed in 1929. It is surrounded by 1,200 acres formerly owned by William Wrigley, Jr., president of Wrigley's Chewing Gum Company. Inspired by one of the world's most celebrated architects, Frank Lloyd Wright, the roof features Arizona copper, and the gold leaf on many of the ceilings adds a note of elegance to this world-renowned hotel.

If you're searching for new teeing ground, the two 18-hole P.G.A.-rated courses will keep your attention.

For golfers' convenience and variety, the Biltmore offers two 18-hole PGA-rated golf courses. The original Adobe Course is a Par 72 and measures 6,783 yards from the championship tees. Winding through citrus-lined fairways and stately mansions and surrounded with an abundance of nature, it offers an enjoyable golf experience.

The new Links Course is a Par 71 measuring 6,397 yards. Though it is shorter than the Adobe it is more difficult because of the hilly terrain. A variety of elevations add scenic and spectacular views of the "VALLEY OF THE SUN" stretching for miles below.

Both courses are perfectly manicured with extremely tight fairways and tricky greens. It's always a delight to be a golfer here as tee times are readily available.

For the twenty-fourth consecutive year, the Biltmore has been awarded five stars, Mobil's highest and most prestigious rating. The hotel is proud to have been a five star winner longer than any other establishment in their area. The hotel has 500 rooms, including the new Terrace Court wing which was completed in September, 1982.

We revisited at Christmas just after the new wing was opened and it was evident to us why they won the Five Diamond Award, in recognition of continued dedication to the highest exacting standards. We enjoyed the Terrace Courts guest room. There are other accommodations ranging in size from 450 to 500 square feet. Suites from 600 square feet and up are available by request. Each room offers the amenities of home. They are done in bright, vibrant colors in quality fabrics and furnishings.

There are several exciting possibilities for epicurean delight:

The Orangerie, for lunch and dinner, is the ultimate in fine gourmet dining. Their own orchestra always soothes your ears and adds a touch of romance. The Gold Room, for breakfast, buffet lunch and table d'hote dinner, features entertainment nightly.

When not enjoying the culinary delights, you may want to try the facilities for tennis, horseback riding, and swimming.

If you love to be pampered and are able to accept the finest in resort travel, I feel the Biltmore is the place for you.

"Enjoy the grand life you so richly deserve"

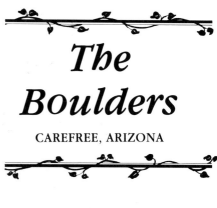

The Boulders

CAREFREE, ARIZONA

"The unspoiled desert"

Located in Carefree, Arizona 15 miles northeast of Phoenix, this new resort is set in the dramatic Sonoran Country desert foothills. The Boulders landscaping accentuates the desert and plant life.

Under the direction of Rockresorts, Inc., the management for many legendary resorts, you can plan on the best. Guest accommodations are individually styled casitas and are sited with a special view and relationship to the rocks and landscape around it. Tastefully decorated with natural wood and Mexican tile, they feature patios and fireplaces.

The Boulders own superb championship golf course consisting of 3-9 holes—your round measures from 5100-6900 yards depending on your tee selection and which 18 holes you play. Jay Morrish of Golforce, Inc., a Jack Nicklaus company, designed the course layout. It is a challenge for champions, but a delight for club players, also. From all parts of the course, memorable views abound and the sunsets are incredible.

Surrounded by jumbo cacti and exotic desert plants, you can remove yourself from the mainstream and really get into your golf. The mountains, fresh air plus the peace and quiet adds to the perfect playing experience.

The clubhouse at the Boulders Club offers excellent dining—Rockresort style—and is open for breakfast, lunch and dinner. Speaking of food, there are three other fine restaurants, each distinctive in menu and decor—

The Palo Verde Room located in the main lodge is a specialty room with a panoramic view of the golf course, serving pleasant and informal dining.

The Latilla Dining Room, also in the lodge, features a front-row view of a waterfall and huge boulder pile for which the resort is named.

The cuisine and service in this formal dining room reflects only the highest Rockresort standards which have won plaudits and awards from Hawaii to the Caribbean. The Discovery Lounge is formed with natural viga and latilla and live entertainment will accompany your relaxation and conversation in the lounge each evening.

For the swimmer there are two heated pools. Tennis, anyone??? Six all-weather tennis courts, a jacuzzi, ballrooming and horseback riding add to your other sporting options.

Camelback Inn
Resort & Golf Club
SCOTTSDALE, ARIZONA

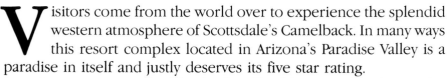

Visitors come from the world over to experience the splendid western atmosphere of Scottsdale's Camelback. In many ways this resort complex located in Arizona's Paradise Valley is a paradise in itself and justly deserves its five star rating.

Guests are captivated by the hotel's old west and Indian ambience. They're greeted first by the attractive western decor of the lobby, which is popular at all times with the guests. It has a homey atmosphere that's softened by trees, baskets of colorful flowers, and antiques.

Guests stay in lovely adobe casas which are scattered among the beautifully landscaped grounds. Everywhere you look you'll see flowers, saguaro cactus, and palm trees.

The casas themselves are beautifully appointed. Most are located on the ground level. All have private patios and come complete with built-in bars.

Dining is always a pleasurable experience at the Camelback. Guests can select from four quite different restaurants or opt for a poolside buffet breakfast or luncheon.

The crown jewel of the restaurants is the Chaparral Restaurant which offers diners a breathtaking view of Camelback Mountain. The Navajo Room, which is popular for breakfast, lunch, and dinner, offers a changing daily menu; its decor is typically southwestern. The Cactus Patch overlooks the pool and serves light meals throughout the day.

Two lounges are popular with guests for cocktails and entertainment. The Oasis Lounge, a rustic casual room located at poolside, is enjoyed by many. And La Cantina is one of the most popular night spots for music and dancing in the Valley of the Sun.

The Camelback offers a wide variety of entertainment. We enjoyed a Western Steak Fry that was truly unforgettable. Other events include a 1920s Great Gatsby party that's complete with its own supply of bathtub gin . . . served from the tub . . . and a luau complete with roast Kahlua pig.

Golfers have two 18-hole and one nine-hole pitch and putt courses to select from. The courses are challenging and the quiet desert scenery just adds to the experience.

The 7,030-yard Indian Bend course, designed by Jack Snyder, features gently rolling hills and a backdrop of beautiful Camelback Mountain. The 6,584-yard Padre course is challenging to play; many tournaments are held here. The palm and eucalyptus lined fairways are immaculately manicured. The Quail Hollow Pitch and Putt course located in front of the hotel is always popular with guests.

The Camelback has one asset that most women will enjoy…it's unusually well stocked and fashionable pro shop. I always set aside a kitty so I'll have the pleasure of picking up a few items in this shop. You should, too.

The Camelback has a variety of other recreational activities including hiking, horseback riding, bicycling, and swimming. There's a whirlpool in addition to the swimming pool, something many of us enjoy after a long day on the links.

"Captivating Old West ambiance"

"Totally posh"

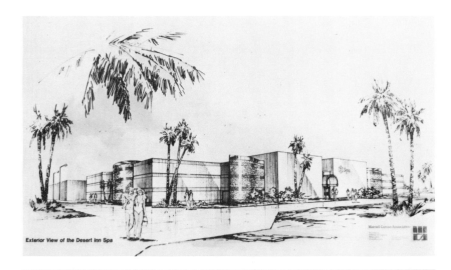

Exterior View of the Desert Inn Spa

At right, the Country Club welcomes guests. Above, the new Desert Inn Spa. When complete, the complex will rival European spas, an exciting addition to already great golf facilities.

Country Club

Certainly this world famous Inn and Country Club is not new to you, but the new look it is taking on will get a grand ovation. In one of the most exciting cities in the world — Las Vegas — plans have been announced to open one of the world's most complete health spas. Known as the "queen" of Las Vegas' famed strip, the newly expanded Desert Inn Country Club and Spa will encompass 18,000 square feet and be totally "posh," rivalling well-known European spas.

The Inn's queenly reputation is justified, since "she" houses 818 guest units, each individually designed and featuring such luxuries as private kitchens, separate formal dining rooms, bars, living rooms and, of course, whirlpool baths. Some even have their own private swimming pools.

Decorated to reflect a variety of themes, I can assure you the accommodations will please even the most particular guest. If you truly want a memorable stay, check into a penthouse suite — seeing is believing — they are breathtaking.

Desert Inn

LAS VEGAS, NEVADA

Golf here is synonymous with the Desert Inn; so much so, in fact, that a special wing has been named for the golfers. The course has plenty of challenge with its large majestic trees, doglegs, and giant lakes. This 7,089-yard course from the blue tees has tested many of golf's greatest players. You may remember it as the original home of the Tournament of Champions (1955–1966), where 10,000 silver dollars were rolled out to the winners in a wheelbarrow. It has also been the site of the Gold Cup International, J & B Scotch Pro-Am, and LPGA Tour events.

One of my favorite pastimes each year, while there with my husband for the Gold Cup, is the wonderful shopping. No place in the world offers more selection.

When it comes time for dining, your taste buds must choose from among seven restaurants. Whatever you do, don't miss the Portofino Room if you enjoy Italian *buon gusto* food. They were recently honored by United Airlines.

For the ultimate in French cuisine, the famed Monte Carlo Room has been the recipient of many awards. Then "Showtime" in the Crystal Room presents top talent twice nightly.

The Inn's president, Burton Cohen, once aptly remarked that "a hotel is like a child who takes on the personality of its parents." In the case of a hotel, the parent is the personnel, and you will love the service and the well-trained staff.

Furnace Creek Inn

DEATH VALLEY, CALIFORNIA

Death Valley is an immense wild land that man has never been able to tame. As we arrived by car, we saw heat waves dance above harsh, white salt while dust devils twisted gracefully across the vast desert floor.

Beyond us were the great mountains into whose rocks incalculable forces have sculpted an incredible story. The climate is the force that has carved Death Valley into the distinctive forms common to deserts around the world.

Having no outlet to the sea, its streams are often encrusted along their banks and are saltier than any ocean. Being miles from civilization in the heart of the wilderness of Furnace Creek seemed like a revelation to me.

One of the highlights of my traveling to play golf was finding it here at Death Valley. For over 50 years, travelers from every walk of life have been enjoying this magnificent Inn, now a California landmark.

At one time, this was a place of sorrow, but as we checked in and went to our luxurious room, I immediately felt that this visit would be a time of pleasure — and it certainly was. The accommodations at the Inn are spacious, Spanish-type villas located on top of a mesa overlooking gardens, the valleys, or the pool. Much enjoyment can be found in these superbly decorated rooms.

At the Ranch Inn nearby, some of the accommodations are on the golf course while others overlook the Ranch swimming pool. There are rustic cabins if you really want to get in the picture of the "Old West."

The 18-hole golf course was designed by William Bell. It poses its own special challenges, but I would not say it is as hard as some. The spectacular setting puts you in touch with nature, surrounding you with trees, flowers, and a few orchards, while rare birds and other wildlife add to your pleasures.

As we were playing, I couldn't help but think of what happened since the borax 20-mule team started their trek. Reflections of past and present come to mind in this desert landscape where superhuman effort plus lots of planning and tenacity have created a playground for people from all over the world.

Overall, this course would be considered "sporty," but one must take it seriously as there is plenty of trouble waiting.

After golf the Corkscrew Lounge is a charmer and very popular, done in the typical style of the "Old West." The Steak House is another

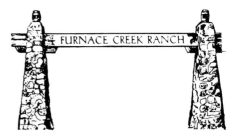

Reflections of past and present come to mind in this desert oasis.

"The Furnace Creek Resort is for exploring"

very popular spot. Served with the salad bar, it's "all you can eat" and then some!

The Inn's superb Dining Room menu is justly renowned as is the Oasis Supper Club. This Fred Harvey resort is famous for service and food that go hand-in-hand.

The Ranch has its own general store and there are many quaint shops to explore. For more entertainment, try swimming, horseback riding, and touring the museums and the desert.

Horseshoe Bay Country Club Resort

HORSESHOE BAY, TEXAS

"One of the world's best kept secrets"

This premier property is located in L.B.J. country, and is truly one of the "best kept secrets in Texas".

Accommodations range from condominiums to luxurious townhouses and private homes. Decorated and furnished so well, they make you feel right at home. Most accommodations have glorious views of the outstanding bay. When we were there we noticed the activity as it seems everyone was having such fun.

The marina is outstanding, and their landmark is the lighthouse—at night the reflection on the bay is great.

We found the food to be exceptional in all three dining rooms. The Captains Quarters serves tableside with gourmet food and service unmatched. The Fairwind serves foods of the state, is a bit less formal and caters to basics, steak, lobster etc.. Harbor Light is very relaxed, play-clothes are permissable.

Imagine 3 championship golf courses to choose from. The Slick Rock golf course is really a favorite of ours. It is a great design by Robert Trent Jones. There are more than 70 traps, and plenty of water. The front nine are wooded, and the back nine are more open with rolling fairways. It is a par 72. Championship yardage is 6,839. Ram Rock is also a championship course and is 6,946 yards. Applerock, just newly opened is a 6,999 yard championship course. It is a perfect blend of the two—the front nine are more flat and the back are hilly.

This is the only course where some of the greens touch the large L.B.J. lake, named after President Johnson. It is very scenic, and from some of the tee boxes it is so scenic it will take your breath away. "The elevation of tees are so high."

Boating, tennis, swimming as well as great trails for horses offer plenty of other sports activities. Another plus, they do have an airport.

If you like to shop there are plenty of quaint shops for another pastime.

If you're looking for something new, look for "the best kept secret in Texas".

"Play golf with the gods"

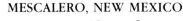

Inn of the Mountain Gods

MESCALERO, NEW MEXICO

If you want to play golf with the "gods," the Mescalero Indian Tribe has developed its Inn of the Mountain Gods as a complete environment for leisure and play. You arrive to a panoramic view of native lands that stretch for miles and miles, an Indian reservation covered with timber-pine, aspen, spruce, and white oak. The Lodge is surrounded by a mirrored lake with the Sierra Blanca Mountains as a backdrop, truly a visual treat to acquaint you with Nature. The Lodge's exquisite lobby is a focal point and enjoyed by all.

A multi-million-dollar complex, the Inn's ultimate goal is to be completely staffed by tribal members.

This resort is designed for the man of leisure, but as we left the golf course, we weren't too sure. The course is a real test of a golfer's skill, but, enhanced by the magnificent setting, not to worry. A Par 71 from the regular tees and 6,419 yards long, it seemed much longer because of the hills and general layout. However, from the championship tees, Par is 72.

Bordering on the lake can be reason for taking plenty of golf balls, too. The real test comes from the numerous traps, doglegs, and over-the-water holes. Of course, the low-handicap golfer will enjoy this layout immensely, but other golfers will love it, too, as the scenic beauty will keep your mind off any shortage of skill.

Our accommodations were spacious and pleasantly decorated with full amenities throughout. Each room offers a sweeping view of the out-of-doors — the lakes, the golf course, and the mountains as well.

When you return from your outdoor sport, they have a perfect indoor one — eating. Charming dining rooms serve the best Southwestern food you have ever eaten, and serve it well with real friendliness. Noted for their pride in making every guest feel special, the Inn is becoming one of the most distinguished resorts in New Mexico.

The Inn is only a few minutes from the famous horse racing at Ruidoso Downs if you're into horses. If you're a ski lover but can't leave your golf long enough, this is the resort for you as it's not uncommon to ski in the morning and golf in the afternoon at the right time of the season with the Sierra Blanca Ski Resort only 19 miles away.

The Inn of the Mountain Gods is 191 miles from Albuquerque where you can fly by Air Midwest. You can also fly from El Paso by Airways of New Mexico. The Inn will happily arrange ground transportation with advance notice.

A popular gathering spot for guests enjoying this focal point in the hotel lobby.

La Costa

CARLSBAD, CALIFORNIA

There is only one La Costa, a pleasure kingdom tucked between the Pacific Ocean and the sun-drenched mountains of Southern California. As a vacation experience, La Costa is awaiting you — the discriminating person.

Our family has enjoyed La Costa for many, many years, and each time we return, we, like others, sense an excitement that never seems to leave this unusual resort. As you ride in a chauffeur-driven limousine, or your own car, you suddenly feel your spirit setting free.

Your eyes behold immaculately groomed gardens and flowers warmed by California sunshine in this "weather capital of the world."

A friendly and courteous staff will welcome you and offer any assistance you may require. La Costa feels that every guest is a special guest, and you will be one, too. La Costa's staff is used to serving celebrities and royalty, and the best in service is second nature to them.

Rooms are spacious and well appointed with all the amenities of home. Luxurious rooms are available in the main hotel building or near the spa and are comfortable and colorfully decorated. You may prefer a sunny cottage on the golf course with a master bedroom, living room, bar, bath, and balcony overlooking the golf course.

Their Chateau Suites or La Costa Villas are the ultimate in luxury.

Speaking of golf, La Costa has an extraordinary golf course with a rare blend of features that satisfy the most demanding golfer. The true gem of the layout is in its versatility which transforms golf into an interesting and challenging, but fair, test. Who knows? A combination of tranquility, scenic beauty, and (almost) ever-present sunshine could lead you to a hot round.

For the past 12 years, La Costa has joined as co-sponsor of "MONY Tournament of Champions."

The beautiful La Costa championship course is a Par 72 and 6,911 yards that will test your mettle without intimidating you. The 17th hole is considered a "monster" by the pros. It is 573 yards and a Par 5.

This is a classic course designed by Dick Wilson in the '60's.

Dining is an experience to savor. Superior cuisine is prepared with pride and attentively served in an atmosphere both comfortable and pleasing.

Pisces serves "Delicacies of the Sea" and is one of the finest seafood restaurants we have eaten at anywhere. Coats are required for gentlemen. The Seville Room is a quiet, but exciting setting for Italian cuisine. We found interesting creations masterfully prepared and served, and you should, too.

The Steak House will tempt your more casual mood, inviting you to build your own salad and enjoy fish, chicken, chops, and steak in a hearty, robust manner. The Tournament Champions Lounge is a famous gathering place, and it is not uncommon to see your favorite star and rap with him or her about your day's game. Last, but definitely not least, the Spa Dining Room has been designed to help you lose weight, and you do lose weight even though the menu features tempting gourmet delicacies.

Speaking of the spa, I could go on and on. The facilities are so complete and the results so good that a book could be written about this subject alone.

Tennis is played on La Costa's fabulous courts and attracts many celebrities. For further adventures, La Costa is 15 minutes from the ever-popular Del Mar Race Track, 40 minutes from San Diego, and just a little further to Mexico. If you're looking for a "best" in California, make it the "La Costa Experience."

"Where the greats of golf compete"

Another bonus, the Orange Course, is a nine-hole, 3,052 yards.

La Quinta Hotel

LA QUINTA, CALIFORNIA

One of America's foremost retreats and landmarks as well, this graceful hotel with its Spanish architecture has remained immune from the hustle and bustle of a big city. Situated on 32 acres of trees, flowers, and beauty, La Quinta offers a vacation retreat you will never forget.

As you arrive through the long, slender drive with impeccably tended, towering trees on each side, you will immediately feel the pride taken in preserving this exquisite property.

Reminiscent of the early 1900's, the lobby is done in a warm, intimate, but friendly manner, and you can't help noticing its graciousness when you check in. This is just the beginning: wait until you arrive at your accommodation.

Whether you choose a cottage with the charm of the 1920's (with modern conveniences) or one of the newly constructed Spanish-styled cottages, you will find each room tastefully decorated. Some even have their own fireplaces and lanais. You may select singles or doubles; they will be perfect. A private, elegantly furnished home may also be to your liking and they are available. The surrounding trees, shrubs, and flowers assure you of privacy and beauty.

La Quinta Hotel has always been recognized for superb food and services, and to prove it, they have received the Triple AAA Four-Diamond Award, and Mobil Guide rated them outstanding — "worth a trip." *Palm Springs Life* presented them with a Gold Medal Award. I can second all. Dining is always a treat in the Main Dining Room or La Mirage. If you enjoy leisurely dining with a musical background, served by waiters and captains trained in the European tradition, this is a "must."

Four lounges add the extra spark for your spare time. La Cantina

A personality of ever-changing moods adds fascination to this award-winning resort.

is for quiet conversation and relaxing, while the Santa Rosa Room is the cabaret, where entertainment and dancing go as long as you do.

The Golf Club has just the right food and drinks for any golfer, and the Pro Shop has just the right thing for your golfing needs. This Pro Shop, I must say, is far above average.

When you're ready to play golf, you will be totally intrigued with this outstanding course. Recently rated by the Southern California Golf Association at 74.4, it is tough even for the touring pros. The course was designed by Pete Dye, one of the world's most creative and highly publicized architects.

The beauty of the course lies in the fact that the luscious green fairways and some of the greens are right at the base of the Santa Rosa Mountains. The personality of this ever-challenging course changes because of the extreme elevation changes, incorporating all the desert's natural terrain. From the championship tees, the yardage is 6,307 but seems to play much longer. Doglegs, many traps, and water can contribute to your nightmare, but good advice is just to keep your head down and keep swinging.

"Privacy and elegance continue to attract business, political leaders and celebrities"

Three swimming pools and spas grace the grounds. Tennis and bicycling are popular sports. Another favorite pastime could be to count the stars (no, not in the sky, but your favorite showbusiness personalities — or a President). For years, because of the privacy and solitude that this congenial resort exudes, La Quinta has been host to them all.

Located 127 miles from Los Angeles and only 19 miles from Palm Springs, this is recommended for a top spot on your list of "musts."

Gaining prominence in the golfing world, there's only one La Quinta.

The Lodge at Pebble Beach

PEBBLE BEACH, CALIFORNIA

At Pebble Beach, man and nature have teamed up to create an unparalleled golfing experience. Guests of Lodge have privilege of playing Spyglass Hill, above. Every golfer should play it! At right, view of the Lodge from the 18th hole.

More than 100 years ago, Charles Crocker established a tradition of excellence at the Lodge at Pebble Beach. Since the Lodge is located at the heart of a 7,000-acre preserve, you enter through the famed Del Monte Forest and travel the Seventeen Mile Drive. On the way, you'll pass towering pines, cypress trees, craggy rocks, pounding surf, lush gardens, and magnificent homes. Then, as you skirt the legendary links of Pebble Beach, you arrive at the doors of the Lodge.

The accommodations are comfortably spacious and offer a soothing tranquility, yet are a perfect complement to the Lodge's majestic surroundings.

How well I remember playing golf in May when the weather was perfectly temperate and yet mellowing at night. But such fun in the evening enjoying the fireplace.

Dining spells contentment, whatever your desire. You may try the flickering candlelight of Club XIX, the intimate Restaurant Francais, or Evening at the Lodge in the chandeliered dining room where crystals shimmer alongside masterfully served California cuisine prepared by fine culinary artists.

After dinner, you may delight in music and dance in the dining room, or enjoy a nightcap at Club XIX. The Tap Room is casual, but is a

classic restaurant serving traditional fare. And last but not least is the Gallery, an informal family-style restaurant overlooking the first tee.

 The golf course here is rated as one of the top five courses in the world. You can test your skills on a championship course where nature and man have teamed up to create an unparalleled golfing experience. Reminiscent in challenge and scenic appeal, it is of the genre of St. Andrews. This course was honored by having the 1977 P.G.A. Championship, and the U.S. Open in 1972 and 1982.

You also have the privilege of playing Spy Glass as a guest of the Lodge. It is a Robert Trent Jones course that is one of the three played in the annual Crosby Pro-Am. As a third option, Old Del Monte is available. It was the first golf course built west of the Mississippi. Bet you didn't know that!!!! If you just want to improve your short game, they have a Par 3 course.

As far as providing guests with a variety of sporting facilities, though golf is a way of life here, there are 14 tennis courts, two paddle tennis courts, a fresh water pool, sauna and wading pool, and an equestrian center that is considered the finest in the West. Several trails for hikers and joggers are available; fishing and hunting flourish nearby.

You may recognize this from the U.S. Open, the famed 15th hole.

"One of the top five courses in the world"

Loews
Ventana
Canyon
Resort

TUCSON, ARIZONA

Sprawling across 93 acres in Northeast Tucson, and nestled in the foothills of the picturesque Santa Catalina mountains, this year-around destination resort blends into the natural layout of an un-spoiled desert. Breathtakingly beautiful, it is spectacular to see what has been accomplished here.

Truly a first class resort, it is highlighted by the 80-foot Canyon Waterfall, flowing from the mountain and beneath the hotel to a lake at its dramatic entrance. Accommodations at the Loews Hotel are comprised of 400 luxuriously appointed guest rooms and suites, each with a private terrace.

Elegant dining with new American cuisine offering a fabulous view of Ventana Canyon and the Tucson skyline is a must. Canyon Cafe is more informal, but is is situated in a picturesque window setting.

Flying V Bar & Grill are making a mark with the smoked and barbecue specialities. The Cascade, sunken lobby bar again is quite enjoyable as you are among more dramatic views of the Canyon Waterfall. Bill's Grill is a poolside retreat offering gourmet snacks and great sandwiches.

Aside from the hotel, members and guests are offered club-dominiums at the Golf and Racquet Club for a more intimate accommodation.

The luxury units reflect the standards of elegance and comfort. With a choice of studio apartment to two bedroom/two bath units with lofts, all have a visual charm.

Depicting a time from the by-gone era of the 1920's, this style of living must be a respected tradition—as it combines an atmosphere of an Old World Estate.

Another dining room option is at the Clubhouse, affording both casual and formal dining overlooking the first tee.

Speaking of tees, you will be spellbound as you look over this most spectacular golf course. Imagination and experience was under the able direction of Tom Fazio, the designer. Believe me, you need not only imagination but concentration to play it. #3 hole is the shortest par 3 he has ever created, 107 yards and also the most expensive, as the tees and cartpaths were built by hand.

The 6,969 yards is rated 70.4 from the blue tees. Nine more holes will open November, 1985.

The Lakeside spa is fabulous with a fitness trainer. A complete tennis club plus swimming pools and hot tubs make this a real desert winner.

*A first-class resort
surrounded by
nature's
extravaganzas.*

Because great care was taken to preserve the natural terrain, this course possesses its own distinctive flow and movement across the land.
"Plan on a memorable experience."

As we approached this stunning Inn's *porte cochere,* my husband and I knew it had been much too long since our last visit. What a treat! From the moment we stepped out of our car, we felt a special warmth and sense of welcome.

While checking in, we feasted our eyes on the lobby, richly decorated in a blend of Indian, Mexican, and early California motifs. The furnishings are all custom-designed and accented by priceless antiques of museum quality. Exquisite flowers in huge wicker baskets added a lighthearted accent of color. In the style of an early Spanish home, discreet seating arrangements for conversation, huge fireplaces, and authentic style rugs made us feel welcome to linger.

Pleasing the particular – taste, texture, and eye appeal are unmeasurable.

We found the attitude of the Inn honest and irresistably hospitable. An aura of relaxation suddenly envelops you in such an atmosphere of abiding cordiality.

In the afternoons, a tea is served; also coffee, sherry, and perhaps a *petit four?* For a quiet time, try the Fireside Room as a hideaway.

Everywhere you stroll outdoors, winding pathways will lead you through a variety of garden bowers. Imported statues of bronze and water fountains dot the grounds near conversation areas.

Since the Inn caters to the most demanding tastes, their deluxe rooms, executive suites, one- or two-bedroom suites, or the Palacio and Castillo suites are par excellence.

Entering your VIP suite, you will enter a world of uncompromising comfort. Discover the built-in bar, whirlpool, and private courtyard for catered entertaining and relaxing.

 Golf at Rancho Bernardo can make some aspects of your game pleasantly predictable. Days are consistently balmy, with just enough afternoon breeze to tamper with an otherwise well-placed shot.

The Par 72 West Course is breathtakingly beautiful as it rolls down the valley like a great green ribbon. Though only 6,400 yards, it is deceptive in that each shot must be played with rifle-like accuracy.

Be careful of the strategically placed traps as well as the lakes, streams, bunkers, and doglegs. They will test your talent. The links themselves are landscaped in trees, pines, and super-lush greens.

The championship character of the course is evident with almost every hole, but we especially found the 18th hole of tournament class laced with sudden-death subtleties. As for their pro shop, it is as exquisite as the surroundings.

Besides the West Course, 27 more holes at Oaks North Executive Course are available for guests of the Inn.

As for fine dining, two restaurants with character and impeccable cuisine are yours to enjoy.

El Bizcocho is a mezzanine lounge. La Taberna is for sipping a cocktail before dinner as you enjoy the semi-classical harpist.

The main dining room offers a selection of 16 entrees and 350 labels of fine wine from California and around the world. Your captain and waiter will give excellent service, attending to your every desire. The end result of this combination of taste, texture, and eye appeal is unmeasurable.

The Veranda for breakfast and lunch offers a more casual, but pleasant atmosphere. After five, the feeling changes to sophistication with candlelight dining and menus for the most expert connoisseurs.

After dinner, try La Bodega lounge for evening entertainment and dancing.

We will always savor our experiences at Rancho Bernardo, and I hope you will, too.

"An atmosphere of abiding cordiality"

Rancho Bernardo Inn

SAN DIEGO, CALIFORNIA

Rancho de los Caballeros is a perfectly quiet world set amid 20,000 acres of wondrous beauty where a day is not measured by the tyranny of hectic schedules or clocks, but by the swirling mass of silent, peaceful moments spent in reflecting on a new discovery.

The challenging golf course, adjacent to the property, offers guests complete freedom to play as much golf as they desire.

This is a new golf resort, relatively unheard of until lately. Rumor has it that it is gaining in popularity.

The excitement begins as you approach this "Ranch of Gentlemen" and notice its air of leisure and relaxation. Despite its newness, the aura of an old Spanish heritage is apparent.

The 18-hole golf course is, naturally, of championship calibre, rated 74.1. It features a new clubhouse, pro shop, and dining room. The unique feature that excited me about Rancho de los Caballeros was a feeling of near-seclusion. Mind you, you have to be a desert lover because this is the essence of peacefulness and privacy. It combines complete serenity with natural beauty to fulfill a promise of paradise.

The present motif of Spanish and western influences blends naturally with the outdoor environment. Varied recreational pursuits are basking in the sun, swimming, tennis, and trap skeet shooting.

Accommodations are spacious and the authentic influence of the west is a consistent theme.

Identifiable dinners are served in a ranch-style dining room. Special evening magic materializes nightly in the form of appealing homestyle cooking. And the lounge offers the comforts of your own home, with all the amenities.

Located just outside Wickenburg, Arizona, Rancho de los Caballeros is 55 miles from Phoenix. The Wickenburg Municipal Airport is located just three miles from the ranch, and it is suitable for private aircraft.

If you want to recapture the spirit of discovery, I highly recommend this Rancho.

Rancho de los Caballeros

WICKENBURG, ARIZONA

"Ranch of gentlemen — bring your boots"

The Resort Spa at Tucson National Golf Club

TUCSON, ARIZONA

In the soft foothills of Tucson's Santa Catalina Mountains lies a new resort spa at the Tucson National Golf Club, approximately ten minutes from downtown.

Tucson is exploding with building growth and it is no different at this resort.

Surrounded by 650 acres of pristine Arizona desert, the guest accommodations feature 170 deluxe villa suites surrounded by the golf course, offering breathtaking views from the patios and balconies.

Each tastefully decorated and refurbished you can feel right at home. With a casual elegance their guests unwind and enjoy this veteran "old western town".

There are three cocktail lounges for your thirst and two restaurants including a beautiful gourmet room.

Boasting 27 holes of championship golf, actually comprising 3-9 hole layouts. The Orange/Gold (#1 course) is a par 73 and from the blues measures 7100 yards. The Orange/Green (#2 course) is par 72 from the blue is 6,692 yards and is rated 72.9. Gold/Green (#3 course) is a par 73 yardage from the blue is 6,860 and the rating is 74.6.

The original course was designed in 1960 by Robert Bruce Harris, and the Green course was constructed in 1980. The Orange course was remodeled in 1981 as well as the Gold course in 1983.

The golf course encompasses 10 lakes and 188 traps.

This is the Western Home of Golf Digests Instructional Schools and for years they hosted the Tucson open.

After a day on the links you may wish to take a side trip to heaven as you journey through the new spa opening 1986. "You are promised the ultimate."

There is a tennis center plus 2 swimming pools and Hydrotherapy pools. The building of their convention center along with the new spa is happening at this writing...

When you think fun, relaxation and great golf...don't forget this place.

The Resort Spa at Tucson National Golf Club "Could be a side trip to Heaven."

Sheraton Tucson El Conquistador

TUCSON, ARIZONA

The new luxurious 440-room Sheraton El Conquistador located in Tucson, Arizona, is one of the newest and largest in the Southwest. It is impressively situated in the foothills of the Santa Catalina Mountains.

 The challenging 27 holes of golf were designed to keep the interest of the low handicapper as well as that of the amateur.

The 18-hole, 7,085-yard Par 72 course is adjacent to the hotel, and surrounding it are the newest nine holes designed by Jeff Hardin and Gregg Nash of Phoenix, Arizona. It is known to be a fun course, though demanding. If you are used to playing on fairly level courses, the changes in elevations here, because it has been designed as a mountain-style course, might be deceptive.

Gullies, ravines, and saguaro cacti are some of the natural hazards that complement the bunkers and water hazards that were integrated into the course.

In addition to the golf, guests are offered tennis, horseback riding, racquetball courts, swimming, jogging trails, and the use of a year-round health club. No matter how beautiful it is, I recommend that you miss the heat of summer for some of these activities.

Food in the various dining rooms is served with the great style of the "Sheraton touch." You will certainly enjoy the feeling of the Old West, as your accommodations are reminiscent in decor.

If you like the desert, golf, and a luxury resort, then this is one of the Southwest's finest hotels for you. The dry desert air, along with sparkly sun and no crowds make this a haven for "peace, rest, and relaxation" — but in this Spanish decor you can be transported back to the early days and reminiscing can be as much fun as your vacation.

"One of the newest and largest resorts in the Southwest, featuring desert, golf, and luxury"

Silverado

NAPA VALLEY, CALIFORNIA

Amongst gentle hills, ancient oaks and groves, and in a boundless maze of Napa vineyards, lies a most secluded and sophisticated resort. As you arrive at this stately mansion, the atmosphere is both impressive and inviting. French and Italian architecture have been combined to complement the surrounding natural beauty. Immediately you can feel the spirit of a special vacation in a spot made for golfers.

Though Silverado has a capacity for more than 450 guests, you are insured total privacy while enjoying your accommodations. Whether you choose a one-, two-, or three-bedroom suite, you will find warm, inviting decor with private walkways, pools, and hidden courtyards. The grounds are alive with flowers of the season and accented by palms.

Two very fine golf courses await your playing pleasure; both have been designed by Robert Trent Jones and are arched with trees. There are plenty of traps, beautiful greens, and lush fairways. It has been said that no matter how you play at Silverado, you are going to win a "five-mile walk through Paradise," with 360 acres laced with lakes and ponds, plus three sweetwater creeks. Add to this the beauty of the redwood, oak, and madrone and 200-year-old eucalyptus, blending with the Napa woodlands.

Making your golfing experience here one to remember, the South Course is 6,500 yards long with deceiving side hill lies and over a dozen water crossings.

The North Course stretches 6,700 yards, but it is occasionally forgiving. A demanding course, with plenty of trees for troublesome moments, but with all the surrounding beauty, it is really hard to be troubled for long on this enjoyable layout. Silverado was honored by the National Groundskeepers Association, so you can guess what a treat you are in for as you play among lush greens and manicured fairways.

The lively and exceptionally well-stocked pro shop does an excellent job of buying for the needs of their guests, and it is a showplace for golfers.

In the valley known for fine wines, Silverado restaurants are known for fine foods. The Royal Oak is the vintage restaurant overlooking the gardens. Here the mood is as mellow as the menu. The Royal Oak is considered one of the valley's best for dining and wining.

The Silverado Dining Room is a chandeliered salon, where California cuisine is served by candlelight. The Silver Bar and Grill is for your more casual moments, offering great food and overlooking the North Course. The Patio Terrace Lounge is always a popular spot. With all of these dining options, Silverado is sure to please even the most demanding culinary craving.

Silverado is a total destination, and they even have a multi-million-dollar conference center.

If you would like to swing the racquet as well as the club, you'll find that Silverado is into tennis in a big way. Biking, swimming, and horseback riding are other popular sports and pastimes here. You won't want to miss a trip through the wine country, and the resort will be happy to arrange your tour.

Temperature is a favorable factor, averaging around 72 degrees.

This 1,200-acre estate nestled in the heart of California's wine country features two Robert Trent Jones golf courses.

"Secluded, sophisticated hideaway"

Walden on Lake Conroe

LAKE CONROE, TEXAS

"This beautiful championship course calls for fresh tactics"

Taking advantage of the 22,000-acre Lake Conroe, this fine resort is fun-filled. Walden is tucked away in Montgomery County, approximately one hour's drive north of Houston. Commanding a majestic presence on beautiful blue Lake Conroe, it is a perfect setting for a memorable experience.

Your accommodations will be spacious, and luxuriously decorated condominiums and townhouses situated near the lake and golf course. You may choose from one, two, or three-bedroom condominiums in a wooded setting.

Dining is a pleasure in the magnificent Commodore Dining Room of the Walden Yacht Club, reflecting a panoramic view of the

The 22,000-acre Lake Conroe provides a beautiful setting for golf or for restful relaxation.

lake and land. Their varietal menu is extensive and will assure you a perfect dining experience.

For your casual dining, the 19th Hole restaurant at Walden's Golf Center serves Texas-style bar-b-que, as well as delicate *hor d'oeuvres* and elegant banquets.

 The Walden championship golf course was designed and engineered by the internationally known golf course architectural firm of Von Hagge & Devlin, Inc. The popular Bruce Devlin is their Director of Golf.

The 18-hole championship course is 6,797 yards long, a Par 72. It is a complete departure from the usual and accepted form of a golfer's tactical examination. The 11th hole is a 580-yard Par 5, double dog leg onto an island green. Many trees, plenty of water, and multitudes of traps command your attention. Perfectly tended greens and well manicured fairways are only part of the fun here, and water lovers will find water everywhere, sparkling and blue.

Other recreational facilities include tennis, sailing, water skiing, fishing, swimming, boating, and bicycling. Walden is known, too, for their 520-slip marina, one of the largest in Texas.

Limousine service from Houston Intercontinental Airport is available by request, and private aircraft may use Montgomery County Airport, 20 miles from Walden.

Whether your desire is for a fun-filled vacation or a successful business conference with golf, Walden has thought of everything.

The Wigwam

LITCHFIELD PARK, ARIZONA

Discriminating guests never tire of this premier resort which has received the coveted Five Star Mobil Award and Triple A's Five Diamond Award. Year after year, the same clientele return, including us.

Your warm welcome upon arriving at the doorstep is only a glimpse of what is ahead. The aim is to make you feel right at home, but with added extra enhancements such as luxurious surroundings and beautiful sights.

Golfers will be challenged by three unusual 18-hole championship courses. The Gold Course, build by Robert Trent Jones, plays 7,220 yards from the championship tees. The Blue Course, with many water holes and narrow-lined fairways, awaits you with lots of sneaky little traps. Somewhat shorter than the Gold Course, the Blue Course is a Par 70. The West Course plays 6,861

yards and is demanding for any golfer. There is never a problem getting on as a guest. They will cater to your tee time requests and the Pro Shop's friendly staff will cater to your every whim.

The beauty of the Wigwam golf experience is the natural setting with only the desert as its backdrop. This, plus the well tended greens and lush fairway that demand a lot of attention for a desert course, will assure you a fair round of golf.

Superbly appointed guest rooms match every taste. You may choose an opulent suite, complete with living room. Or an executive bedroom with patio and dressing room. Or a private bungalow. Or a modest room. All are decorated tastefully and with distinctive charm.

Evenings are always exciting at the Wigwam. Music fills the air. The service is unobtrusive, a sign of elegance and pride, underscoring the latest in fine and exclusive cuisine. The Owl Lounge features exotic atmosphere and tidbits for the adventurous.

The most popular sport at the Wigwam is golf, naturally. Tennis follows as a close second. For a change, you may wish to ride horses, swim in the spacious pool, or sunbathe. A lovely spa is a comfortable place to relax with saunas, massage facilities, beauty salons, whirlpools, and exercise equipment.

You will feel the caring and quality of the Wigwam in all their endeavors. It will become immediately apparent why they are one of the few resorts in America to receive these outstanding awards for excellence. In my book they have earned all the awards justly.

"They will cater to your tee time requests"

Woodlands Inn and Country Club

THE WOODLANDS, TEXAS

The Woodlands Inn and Country Club might well be called Tranquility Base. Located just 25 miles north of Houston, it's worlds away from that bustling city.

The Woodlands just feels remote. The wooded grounds are landscaped with winding lakes, graceful waterfalls, tall Texas pines. There's a country kind of atmosphere about the place, a peacefulness that's rather enjoyable.

Nowhere is this more obvious than in the guest rooms, which consist of one and two-bedroom suites, with individual study areas and other amenities. The suites are arranged mostly in two-story lodges, so the feeling is very private.

You must experience dining at the Glass Menagerie, one of the finest restaurants in the area. The view, the ambience, and the cuisine all add up to one memorable experience. The restaurant is set on the wharf overlooking the shimmering lake and waterfall. The soft music of violins is a dining accompaniment. The cuisine is special here, too. You'll enjoy chateaubriand, snapper, freshly baked breads and pastries, baked Alaska. And there is entertainment nightly.

T-Lautrec is the other restaurant at the Woodlands. It's much more casual but it also has a view of the lake, and the food is very good.

The Inn's two 18-hole golf courses were conceived and designed by internationally respected golf architects. They offer a mixture of fun and challenge. The East Course and newest is a Devlin von Hagge layout; it's short but difficult because there are obstacles such as island greens, heavily trapped and elevated greens, water blocking 10 holes and completely surrounding the 13th green.

If you need some advice on how to play this difficult layout ask the resort's director of golf, Mancil Davis, who at 29 years of age held the world professional record of 43 holes in one.

Though you are away from the congestion, you are only 15 miles from Houston International Airport, and the Inn will assist you with limousine service.

Twenty-four tennis courts are waiting for you, and they have one of the greatest health spas, offering Roman pools, saunas, steam room, massages, facials, and herbal wraps. Hiking or biking, swimming or horseback riding, ice skating or fishing — you can't miss at the Woodlands Inn.

If you want to play golf, be pampered, and r

"Ambiance,
cuisine,
service—
a memorable
experience"

THE WOODLANDS INN
AND COUNTRY CLUB

sen a priority resort.

Mauna Kea

KAMUELA, HAWAII

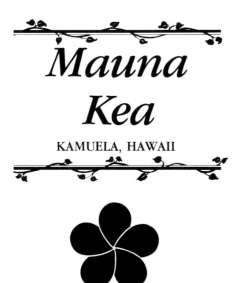

A graceful layout, this world-renowned course sports smashing ocean views and grandiose beauty. Third hole, above, and 11th hole, right, are justly famed highlights.

"A complete destination"

Mauna Kea welcomed its first guest in 1965, the most lavish hotel ever built in Hawaii. Located approximately 170 air miles southeast of Honolulu, it commands breathtaking views of the Kahala Mountains and Mauna Kea, the extinct volcanic mountain which gave the hotel its name.

Designed as a complete destination resort with the utmost privacy, Mauna Kea's interior walkways and courtyards are open to the refreshing tradewinds and gardens. The beautifully landscaped grounds display plants from the hotel's own nursery, and they have won wide recognition.

Most people think of Mauna Kea as the perfect way of life: attendants, waiters, and personnel are in bright Hawaiian clothing; beautiful flower arrangements everywhere; priceless Asian and Pacific arts and artifacts, which are visible throughout the buildings and grounds. Handmade quilts adorn the corridor walls and each guest room is colored by large floral lithographs created by various Island painters. The tropical fruits sent to your room — all the surprise toiletries, plus your own personal kimono — make you feel "they care."

Dining presents many mouth-watering opportunities in several different settings. The Dining Pavilion, for example, is a free-standing structure seating 300 people on three levels. Two immaculate kitchens prepare continental, American, and international cuisine for the most selective gourmand.

The Garden Pavilion, also free-standing, seats 160 and is very similar in food and service to the Dining Pavilion. The Batik Room, accommodating 180, is extremely popular and advance reservations are suggested. Its unusual interior dining salon was inspired by the "houdah," the canopied throne-like litter used by Asian royalty while riding on the backs of elephants.

Adjoining the Batik Bar is a separate, quiet cocktail lounge and outdoor dancing terrace. The Cafe Terrace seats 300 for lunch and overlooks Kaunaoa Bay. The Hau Tree Terrace serves simple fare and light luncheons, and the 19th hole offers beverages and a golfer's menu.

Focusing on the 18-hole golf course, designed by Robert Trent Jones, every golfer will agree there is only one Mauna Kea. All 7,101 yards Par 74 have views of the Pacific from almost every green. The world-renowned 3rd hole is as testy as one could bargain for, while the 11th hole is probably the most difficult of the Par 3's. This course, because of its physical beauty, is enjoyed by all, but to a serious golfer it also offers plenty of demanding challenge.

Bound by a tradition of quality, service, and comfort, the management and staff are always catering to your whims, making this "home" an unforgettable occasion.

I'm always nostalgic for Mauna Kea when we leave and am constantly reminded that the dream of gracious service can still be obtained if you want to pay the price.

Mauna Lani Bay Hotel

KAWAIHAE, HAWAII

Above, seventh hole of the spectacular course designed by Homer Flint on the flanks of the volcano Mauna Kea. Mauna Lani is fast becoming recognized as one of the finest and most elegant resorts in Hawaii.

While it is perched on the ocean's edge of the Kahala Coast on Hawaii's "big island," this hotel would be at home anywhere in the world.

At first glance, a sense of exclusivity clings to this exciting, beautiful structure. Arriving at the doorsteps in itself is a treat. The dramatic atrium with waterfalls and flowers opens its arms wide to you as you are welcomed with a fresh flower lei and escorted to your room by a charming attendant who is most eager to please you.

Once in your elegant and plush room made up of ordinary details carried out to extraordinary lengths, you know that you have arrived in the home of quality. All the amenities I expected were present, and more, even to the fresh flowers in the rooms.

Our first night, we were just in time to please our palates at the Third Floor Restaurant which is fast becoming recognized as one of the finest dining rooms in Hawaii. There is not enough that could be said for the presentation other than "perfect!" The food was elegant and the menu extensive. The service, of course, was attentive and every detail was carried out in the most intimate style.

The Bay Terrace has a bill of fare that changes nightly and the Terrace overlooking the sparkling blue ocean is great, not only for a breakfast or a luncheon feast, but for your eyes to feast on as well.

 "The scenery absolutely commands your attention"

You can't help but admire the natural surroundings of this heroic environment where you are caught between the ocean and the massive flanks of the volcano Mauna Kea. But when you see the volcanic side of the golf course, where the rough happens to be in fantastic lava shapes, you start envisioning what happened here.

Personally, I shot one of my best golf games ever, but had I not, I would not have blamed it on anyone or anything except the scenery. It absolutely commands your attention, it is so breathtakingly beautiful. Every detail is looked after, and the grooming is meticulous, which makes this one of the most outstanding courses in the world. A real must for any player, and may I add, a real challenge.

Country Club Golfer magazine has called it "an astonishing experience," and I can't agree more. Once you have played it, the memory will linger forever. It is a Par 72, 6,800 yards long, and designed by Homer Flint.

The professionally equipped pro shop and clubhouse plus another restaurant adjacent to the golf course are ready to serve your every whim. This restaurant serves nightly for casual needs and is also open for breakfast and lunch.

The Tennis Garden has 10 champion courts. Take your pick of swimming, sightseeing or playing on the candy-white beaches, or just plain relax and enjoy.

Sheraton Molokai

MOLOKAI, HAWAII

We never realized that we were "dauntless tropic adventurers" until our last visit to the Hawaiian Islands. With great excitement, I want to share this refreshing resort with you. If you are ready to step back in time, this can be a haven for you, too.

Molokai, known as the Friendly Isle today, was once called the Lonely Isle for the power of its "kahunas" (priests) who practiced sorcery. They were much feared throughout the island chain.

Somehow, on our previous trips to Hawaii, we overlooked Molokai. Like others, we associated it only with the leper colony. We found it to be a secluded, innocent, untouched, and ruggedly beautiful land only a 25-minute flight by commuter airline from Oahu. Dozens of flights per day make it a convenient and easy trip.

Upon our arrival, we were met by a scheduled shuttle van. As we rode, we passed the area where you may take a safari tour through the Exotic Wildlife Kingdom. Here deer, kudu, impala, giraffe, antelope, and pheasant roam free. Our driver told us that he had grown up practically in the Kingdom; this was before they started charging an entry fee.

Before deciding whether or not to cram in another island visit, we heard the accommodations were thatched huts and ceiling fans. We weren't sure we were ready for that atmosphere. Much to our surprise and delight, we found our hut to be luxurious and decorated in excellent taste. It was spacious, warm and homey; immediately we felt much better.

Each cottage has a private lanai overlooking rolling green lawns and the sparkling blue ocean.

There are two dinner houses, one called the Paniola Broiler with a hearty ranch-style fare of steaks served in the spirit of "Old Hawaii," fresh fish caught close by, and a complete salad bar. We enjoyed the Ohia Lodge also, which seemed to bring visitors and islanders together for dining and Hawaiian music.

As we danced into the night, we realized that we would always savor this relaxed pace, one we haven't known for some time.

"Wouldn't you rather be riding a mule on Molokai?" We've all seen the familiar bumper sticker, but quite frankly, I'd rather be playing golf on their championship Par 72 Kalua Kai Golf Course. It is a challenging 6,599 yards long. Designed by Ted Robinson, it is one of the most spectacular and unusual courses we have played. Often compared to the finest Monterey peninsula courses, it features elaborate landscaping. Five holes play alongside rocky ocean cliffs, with many ocean views from several other holes. We remember the wonderful smells of the many island flowers which color and perfume the course. Nature herself really designed the course, states Ted Robinson. Wild turkey is found not only behind the bar, they roam by the dozens over the course along with bright red birds, quail, and doves. Deer are not uncommon, too.

If you want a change of pace, there is swimming, bathing in the lava ponds, and endless numbers of unspoiled white beaches.

Discover the island where the 20th Century is just dawning. It's truly a small island with a big "Aloha!"

"Combines the past and the present"

touffer's Wailea Beach is "a place apart," and a total destination representing all the beauty and luxury Hawaii can offer. We felt a warm "*Aloha!*" as we arrived at Maui's only winner of the Five Diamond Award, which features acres and acres of lush gardens, flowers, and lawns.

It was night-time when we arrived. It looked even darker to us, since it was the only time in our many years of travelling that our luggage had been lost. Our first reaction was "just to get sooo maddddd," but as we entered the magnificent open-air lobby with orchids blooming everywhere and the pleasant attendants at our side, our perspectives changed.

After wandering through the gracious gardens down to the oceanfront, we approached our room with a positive outlook. As we entered, we saw fresh orchids on the pillow and adjusted our moods to correspond with the sweetness of the color and smell.

Of course, the bathroom had a basket of amenities that we were grateful for.

Stouffer's Wailea Beach

WAILEA BEACH, HAWAII

"A place apart"

For golfing, you have an option of playing the Blue Course or the Orange Course.

Our first day, we played at 7:00 a.m. on the Orange Course. I'll bet you wonder how we could play without our clubs and clothes. (As a matter of fact, we did go to the pro shop to cancel our tee time.) Well let me tell you, I rolled up my pants (made great-looking knickers), arranged my shirt, and rented shoes and clubs. I would give them a gold putter for their efforts. It is almost unheard of to have size 11-A shoes for my dear husband, but they had them. Along with the clubs. We were immediately swinging.

Fran, the pro who is such a sweetheart, has put so much care and imagination into everything that even the rented bags were blue and orange in combination to coordinate with the course. Everything has been carried out in a meticulous manner to keep the guests happy.

And speaking of happy, just wait until you play two of the most beautiful courses ever. The grooming is impeccable, with the right amount of challenge and terrific views, and of course the weather was perfect.

The Silver Crescent beach is only footsteps from the Orange Course which is surrounded by the sparkling surf splashing on the shoreline and the gentle mountain slopes which offer some of the finest golf we have ever played.

We felt we had to explore our secluded Eden on the jewelled Hawaiian island of Maui and I'm sure you will, too.

For your dining adventures, you may choose Raffles, the award-winning restaurant featuring continental cuisine and a complete wine list. You'll love the Aloha service and the unequalled setting, surrounded by fine antiques and artifacts, crystal, etched windows, and candlelight, all of it reminiscent of a by-gone era. It overlooks re-

splendent gardens of flowers, offering what can be the most memorable evening of your life.

For lunch, we tried the Maui Onion, adjacent to the pool, which started with Maui onion rings (like no others). Breakfast was perfectly delightful in the Palm Court, which also offers an international buffet each evening. Sunset Terrace is the focal point for winding down at the end of a fun-packed day, with mellow music and a spectacular show by Mother Nature.

If you're still in the mood in the wee hours of the morning, there is the Lost Horizon for cool cocktails, music, and entertainment.

Besides swimming, jacuzzi soaking, sailing, and the beach, you can play tennis on a 14-court Tennis Club which features a tournament stadium.

This is a must in your plan of resort destinations. Aloha!

International Resorts

Saint Geran

MAURITIUS, SOUTH AFRICA

A private slice of Paradise

S urrounded by powder-soft white beaches, this private slice of paradise is fringed with exotic palms, the spectacular Saint Geran lies on the tropical island of Mauritius. Flanked on one side by the coral reefs which transforms the Indian Ocean into a translucent coastal lagoon, and smooth waters of a natural bay.

Designed to blend with the atmosphere of the enchanting island, the hotel is fabulous. Offering a unique lifestyle, it is elegantly casual. All 169 rooms are attractively furnished with patios and balconies just a stones throw away from the beach.

Meals are served on the Terrace Restaurant overlooking the cone-thatched cocktail bar, the pool, dance floor and gardens. The mood is always relaxed, no ties or jackets.

The cuisine is the finest Chinese, Indian, French and Creole dishes, succulent seafood plus lots of exotic fruits. The Pau and Virginie satisfies any gourmet. The casino bar is within the flip of a martini olive from the casino itself.

The Mzamba Grill, where you can linger over your meal, and Pebbles for a bite between bets is a good choice. The Lagoon serves drinks in a breathtaking backdrop.

The 9-hole golf course was designed by Bobby Trent Jones, Junior, and is of championship caliber, with sweeping views of the beautiful ocean, tropical birds, and foliage. It will capture your emotions and try to play havoc with your handicap. Always sunny, but offering a balmy tropical breeze. This course is challenging but enjoyable. Never over-crowded, it is great.

At Saint Geran one lives at jet-set pace, rubbing shoulders with the high rollers and the fastlaners, this is a fairground where casinos, discotheques, restaurants, golf courses, and international gourmet service is an experience you can't describe—''You have to live it'' to enjoy it.

Sun City

JOHANNESBURG, SOUTH AFRICA

*"Home of Golf's First
Million-Dollar
Tournament"*

A millionaire's playground, Sun City has something for everybody. Sparkling theatrical extravaganzas, casinos, and an aquatic wonderworld on a vast man-made lake are only part of the fun awaiting you at this Fun City Resort.

The extensive grounds of this unusual hotel complex are bordered by the untamed wilderness of the Pilanesburg National Park, a game reserve teeming with wild life. Acres of green lawns separate the main hotel from the attractive City Cabananas, a complex that offers excellent family accommodations and has its own restaurants but allows their guests to use all of the hotel's facilities. In addition to the Cabananas is the Main Hotel where luxury rooms await the most discriminating taste, assuring their guests the BEST. All rooms are air-conditioned, have T.V., and overlook the beautiful pool area.

Numerous restaurants can win your palate's favor. For example, the classical Silver Forest, with a pleasing decor of black glass, mirrored walls, and floating chrome trees, offers the finest French cuisine.

Raffles is a "JET SET SUPPER CLUB," complete with dinner and evening entertainment, and, if you are so inclined, after-dinner disco.

Sun City is no doubt a sportsman's paradise, but your true sporting pleasure begins on their challenging golf course. Located in Bopthuthatswana near Johannesburg, South Africa, this course was co-designed by Gary Player and Ron Kirby, and Gary is justly proud of the accomplishment. It is his every dream come true, becoming one of the world's most interesting and popular courses. People are traveling from many nations to enjoy and play here.

Sun City hosted the first million-dollar tournament which, you may recall, was won by Johnny Miller in a sudden-death playoff. Gary Player confirms that this is also one of the most intriguing courses you can play. It is not uncommon to be teeing up while having a Rhino gaze at you and, perhaps, distract you a bit.

Because playing from the longest tee is 7,033 yards, exacting shots can be plenty helpful. Although the distinctive fringed traps are unassuming, they offer a challenge in getting out gracefully. The layout of this unusual but well-designed course will undoubtedly command your talents, but it probably will be a favorite of yours as it is with many others.

"A man-made wonderland bordering on an untamed wilderness"

The winning sounds of bells ringing, lights flashing, luck and laughter highlight the contrasts available at this pleasure kingdom and ring a magical note to a fun-filled golfing vacation in FUN CITY, located only 30 minutes by air from Johannesburg. Other attractions include lawn bowling on two magnificent greens, a complete squash complex, and swimming.

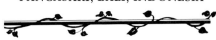

Bali Handara

PANCASARI, BALI, INDONESIA

Among one of the world's greatest golf courses. It sits in an extinct volcano.

Bali Handara is the ultimate getaway, and certainly one of the most interesting resorts in the world.

Small, cozy and comfortable it is situated 3,700 feet above sea level, with the average temperature of 16-20 degrees celcius.

It is approximately one hour ride from Bali, and offers a wonderful insight to the real culture and lifestyles of the Indonesians.

A most charming and intimate cottage can be yours, and will be decorated in the typical decor of their country...You can't help but fall in love with the accommodations, as well as the food...Meals are served in the Kamandala Restaurant and features International cuisine, as well as light snacks or a light refreshment at the snack bar.

Golf Digest has chosen this golf course as one of the world's greatest, and I would have to agree. It is perhaps one of the only golf courses in the world that is set in the crater of an extinct volcano.

This challenging championship course is one hundred hectares of gently sloping tree-line fairways and greens, and is quite interesting to see the greens still being cut and groomed by hand, and then swept with a broom.

Peter Thompson and his associates, Michael Wolveridge, and Donald Fream did an incredible job on design...

It has been said that monkeys roam the course from time to time, and it is fun to hear them call from afar.

Extremely beautiful you can expect to see most any tropical flower you have ever seen. Palms and other tropical trees are everywhere, and if you could imagine yourself in a Garden of Eden it would have to be here. All 6,372 yards. With plenty of water, including views of one of the largest lakes in the area.

A fairly new fitness center is now opened and has all of the right things for one after a hard day on the links.

Local boating and fishing can be arranged on Lake Beratan. Scenic trips to the famous Botanical Gardens, flower and fruit markets are great fun.

Surrounded by rice paddies, the scenery is totally delightful, as is this most UNIQUE RESORT....

Located in the lush green highlands of Central Bali at an altitude of 3700 feet above sea level, with an average temperature of 16 to 20 degrees celcius.

Golf Digest has chosen this among one of the greatest courses in the world.

Bali Hyatt

SANUR, BALI, INDONESIA

Because Bali Handara has only 23 rooms, I felt it apropos to include the traditionally and exclusive Bali Hyatt. Here the most discerning traveler will enjoy his or her stay. It is a world apart and you truly should love the peace and tranquillity.

Situated on the ocean with the warm tropical breezes amidst tropical foliage and the most beautiful 36 acres of landscaped gardens, your every need will be waiting. Every room is newly renovated in light pastels, balinese paintings and teakwood furniture. The service is so personalized. We found our stay here "memorable".

This truly magic island is intriguing and the Bali Hyatt touts five restaurants for your tastebuds. The Spice Islander is a Rendezvous of Bali's elite and is undoubtedly the island's most exclusive restaurant. Here you may enjoy gourmet Indonesian and Western cuisine amongst Balinese decor. The Pizzeria is located on the beach, and the stroll through the gardens to get there is breathtaking. Pizzas, pastas, and authentic Italian delicacies are the specialties.

Fisherman's Place next to the pool is strictly alfresco. Matahari is the regular haunt of Bali's in crowd. You may dance late into the night or sit out on the terrace and enjoy the balmy, tropical weather too.

Though there are only 3 golf holes, it is nice to be able to practice your short game in a park-like setting. We found the 3 holes just a fine place to tune up before our journey to Bali Handara to enjoy their most challenging holes.

If you want a bar, they range from the Piano Bar with lovely music accompanied by the sound of the flowing waters and flower-strewn streams to the Pool Bar, Lobby Bar, Ming Terrace, Beach Bar and the unique Purnama Terrace where you will be entertained by local musicians—no need to be thirsty here!

I felt this hotel was worthy of knowing about, as if you are prone to want to be where the action is and close to the city, shops etc., this is your better choice—downtown. Bali Handara is away from the mainstream and the action. So, whatever your mood, here are the two options I would recommend.

Truly Balinese, you will love the innovative surrounding and definitely feel the culture. The people are very loving and that's the best of all . . .

*Bali Hyatt
Amidst 36 acres of
landscaped
gardens, fronting
the ocean offer
excitement, and
tranquillity.*

Chung Shan Hot Spring Golf Club

PEOPLE'S REPUBLIC OF CHINA

first golf course has placed China on the map for the first time in People's Republic of China

Guests at the Chung Shan Hot Springs Golf Club can enjoy the luxury of the hot springs spa, but just minutes away from the club is Chung Shan Hot Springs Resort. Accommodations include 350 double rooms and independent villas, equipped with a hot springs bathtub. The hotel is not only magnificent to see, but the grounds surrounding it are lush and feature many gardens plus placid lakes.

Chinese and Western food are served in their restaurants, both formal or informal. Highly noted chefs are an important part of their staff. A most gorgeous hotel, everything is met with perfection.

Created by a group of well-known personalities who love golf, this championship golf course of international standard is the first golf course to be built on the mainland China since 1949. Designed by internationally-renowned Arnold Palmer, it has been constructed around the natural landscape and is in perfect harmony with the environment.

It is situated in the Chung Shan Hot Spring Resort in Quangdong Province. Set in a valley, it is surrounded by green paddy fields and imposing mountains.

This 18-hole par 72 course is 5,991 metres, with a unique Chinese feeling. The undulating fairways are comparable to a Scottish links course.

Tennis, shooting, horsebackriding add to your sporting fun; as well as swimming and, of course, sightseeing in the area is intriguing. In just 50 minutes you can jetfoil to Macau from Hong Kong, and then a pleasant 45 minute drive to the club. Prior arrangements can be made by the club staff to handle your transportation.

Discovery Bay

LANTAU ISLAND, HONG KONG

A destination resort across the bay from Hong Kong

Discovery Bay, on Lantau Island, is a short, fast ferry ride from Central Hong Kong. A Golf Club bus awaits you at the ferry pier and transports you to the club 600 feet above sea level.

An 18-hole championship course designed by Robert Trent Jones, Jr. it is surrounded by green hills and panoramic views overlooking the sea, while offering fresh breezes and absolute tranquillity.

You will find during your round at Discovery Bay there is as much a demand that should be placed on the mental approach as the physical work-out. Few of the holes are wide open, and most call for precision and accuracy from the tee. Definitely a course that makes you think. It is a hilly course, extremely beautiful, and includes several breathtaking views, both over the Hong Kong Harbour and inland to the little villages further along the coast of Lantau.

This par 72 championship course is 6,810 yards long, and incorporates a series of lakes that insures year-round watering for the entire course. Designed basically as a walking course, it overlooks a vibrant blue seascape with views of Penang, Chau, and Eastern Lantau. The course spans over 178 acres area. Golfers use easy-to-retrieve floating balls on practice tees.

Recognized as a premier golfing resort, Discovery Bay was host to the Hong Kong Amateur Championship shortly after it was opened.

Discovery Bay is a self-contained township and offers extensive sporting options. Staying at the luxuriously appointed garden apartments or duplex apartments, all with sea views, you have full access to the golf, tennis, squash and racquetball courts, bicycling, canoeing, rowing or windsurfing, walking in the hills or on the beaches and, of course, you can enjoy all the Club facilities. There are shops and banks for your convenience, Chinese and Western restaurants for your enjoyment of good food.

A world apart and yet only a short ferry ride to Hong Kong if you should need the bright lights and exciting bustle of the big city.

Genting
Highlands
Resort

PENANG, MALAYSIA

Welcome to the lofty world of GENTING HIGHLANDS RESORT....Among rolling hills, with lush green jungles and twinkling lights of a city that seems an eternity away, there is much to see and explore.

With three hotels to choose from whatever your needs you are certain to be pleased. We found the Genting Highlands our favorite, and feel the rooms would please the most discriminating tastes. Comfortably, and very well decorated with service to match.

If you choose to go native with your tastebuds you can select from the hot and spicy at the Kampong Restaurant all the while enjoying the atmosphere of ethnic serenity.

The Sails Grill echoes back to the days of the buccaneer and offers exquisite Western and Continental selections. Next door is the Treasure Bar if you should want to sip an aperitif or enjoy an after dinner drink.

The Coffee Terrace is a 24 hour restaurant and has the airy, casual elegance of a Parisan cafe. (Seats 800 people).

The ULU Kali/Library Bar is a cozy rendezvous with soft music to complement your mood.

GENTING HIGHLANDS THEATRE RESTAURANT is one of South East Asia's most spectacular theatre restaurants and serves Chinese cuisine with razzmattazz. International shows are staged live as you enjoy your delectables.

If you really want to move to a beat you may opt for Genting's Discotheque, where the latest sounds and flashing lights can move you to an exciting dimension.

When you play the 18 hole championship course, you will be in for a pleasant surprise if you get up enough courage to play it again. Some golfers consider themselves survivors rather than par breakers.

Designed and built by the able architect firm of Donald Fream Design Group. There were many previous design problems until he came on the scene. Elevation is 3600 feet and is delightfully cool in relationship to the year-round humidity of Kuala Lumpur only 25 miles away.

Plush carpet-like Bentgrass offers golfers an unequaled experience.

Many narrow fairways, ravines, water and extreme ups and downs will lay a challenge out to the best of golfers. Yet the scenery and interest in design will create a memorable experience for all. Many famous golfers have enjoyed these links, and every amenity for your needs can be met in their clubhouse, and pro shop.

Many other exciting happenings can be found, including the Casino de Genting. This exclusive casino is packed with high action and offers friendly and courteous croupiers, well dressed patrons, and in an elegant decor. Blackjack, Keno, Roulette, French Bull, Tai Sai, Baccarat and jackpot machines are exciting levels.

There is a 16-lane bowling facility, indoor heated swimming pool, complete with jacuzzi, plus a wonderful Health Centre including steam rooms, and sauna.

A 800 seat stadium is rife with a multitude of games, tennis, badminton, volleyball, to name a few. Big slides, Amusement centre and theatrette are also enjoyed in an attractive way. Complete with convention facilities, they cater to your every need in "grande" style. If you are looking for the complete getaway with golf #1, and every other choice possible you cannot miss here....

A combination of exciting happenings. Golf, casinos, Health Centre, theaters, tennis etc.

Hakone Prince Hotel

KANAGAWA, JAPAN

Clear blue waters of Lake Ashinoko provide a beautiful view for guests at Hakone Prince Hotel.

Backed by the towering majesty of Mount Fuji, Hakone is a highland resort designed by the famous Japanese architect Togo Murano. The Hakone Prince is historically rich and internationally famous for its many sports activities. Centered around the clear blue waters of Lake Ashinoko, it reflects the awesome majesty of Mount Fuji.

In addition to the main building, guest rooms are available in the Prince Lodge and Prince Cottages. Japanese-style rooms are available in the Ryuguden Annex, should you elect this experience. Because the hotel is circular, every room has a different panoramic view, bringing nature's majesty in focus.

Well decorated, airy, bright and comfortable, there are 296 guest rooms, including the Prince Cottages and Prince Lodge Annex.

The cottages, scattered through the forest that surrounds the hotel, make for a quaint setting. Some of the cottages are built of logs imported from Finland, adding a little different character.

The Prince Hotels have always been famous for their authentic French cuisine, and their beautiful Trianon Dining Room was named for France's Trianon Palace.

The Sakura Restaurant offers a grand view of Lake Ashinoko with a most pleasant atmosphere, and has food to match.

Yamaboshi Coffee House offers an invitation to relax in its comfortably informal room. Club Hinoki features a softly lit room and has the relaxing ambience of a private club.

Dai Hakone Golf Course is a membership club, but guests of the Prince Hotel are eligible to play it. It has been well known to the Japanese golfer as a golf course with long and wide fairways and is located on the hills of Hakone. It is 7,180 yards long and a Par 73. Besides its magnificent setting, it is challenging and extremely interesting. Favoring the long hitter, it is still a fair test of golf for everyone.

Their international conference hall overlooks the classic serenity of a Japanese-style garden, and can accommodate 300 persons. Aside from a five-language interpretation system, they have banquet halls, too.

A specialty shop for your enjoyment, tennis courts, and a swimming pool can add to your pleasure at this spectacular resort. Hakone is located 90 minutes by train and car from Tokyo.

Dai Hakone Golf Course is well known for its long and wide fairways.

"Historically rich and internationally famous"

Hyatt Central Plaza

BANGKOK, THAILAND

Hyatt Plaza Bangkok, is a one billion baht deluxe property, featuring 607 rooms and suites including a Royal Suite, two Presidential suites, four Plaza suites, Executive suites plus the Regency Club. The rooms are outstanding and beautifully decorated, even to the teak, hand-carved wood furniture. Money was not spared and it is evident the moment you walk in.

Walking into the hotel is a joy in itself as it was built to showcase contemporary art. Italian marble, mirror and brass are surrounding a most magnificent waterfall that flows among the greenery and natural surroundings. It is an experience just to sit in the lobby.

The restaurants are truly five star and I recommend them all highly. Hugo's Continental Restaurant happens to be one of my most favored. Service to match the food, and decor that is simply elegant. The Dynasty Chinese Restaurant can compare with any in the world. The open-air Chom Talay Seafood Restaurant overlooking the pool in a terrific tropical setting "is a must."

For entertainment the hotel offers the Lobby Lounge, also the Hollywood Discotheque.

Overlooking Chatuchak Park and the golf course you can see for miles, and speaking of golf the 18 hole championship State Railway course is just across the street. Offering plenty of challenge with the over-abundance of Canals, and other water, anyone can play here and enjoy. Guests of the Hyatt are of course guaranteed Tee Times. Well bunkered with narrow fairways, plenty of trees, and natural beauty add to your assurance of a good round. A par 72 and a championship course the yardage is 6,758 and rated 72.0. You won't want to miss Navatanee, #1 course in Thailand, it is 6,906 yards long, home of the 1975 World Cup. Though it is private, guests of the Hyatt have playing privileges, and the impeccable manicuring is picture perfect.

Located next to one of the largest shopping centers in Asia and only 15 minutes from downtown by expressway, you're sure to enjoy the location, peace and quiet.

Hyatt Central Plaza-Bangkok Located next to one of the largest shopping centers in Asia.

Karuizawa

KARUIZAWA, JAPAN

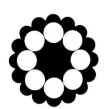

*"A
supermarket
of golf
in an exclusive
setting"*

A popular summer resort for foreign residents and visitors since the Meijis era, this highland area of great natural beauty is now an exclusive world-famous resort. The Karuizawa Prince stands distinguished, surrounded by over 400 rustic cottages scattered through a pine forest. All 530 guest rooms differ in size and style. Suites are unusually large with picture windows offering a panoramic view of the out-of-doors. Suites or V.I.P. suites are perfect because of the tasteful decor and appointments.

Restaurants, such as the Nishiki Chinese Restaurant serving classical Chinese cuisine, could not offer a nicer treat. Or you may enjoy French cuisine and fine imported wines in a romantic softly-lit atmosphere.

Truly a "supermarket of golf," Karuizawa has six courses with exciting challenges for players of any age and capability.

There are three East courses and three West courses, the latter being designed by Robert Trent Jones. The already natural beauty is enhanced by velvety greens and pet smooth fairways, but you can capitalize on these conditions while enjoying to the utmost. The Karuizawa Hotel golf course is located immediately adjacent to the hotel and is 6,331 yards long. This Par 72 course is open from April 1 to November 30. An additional nine-hole short course is available for putting or smoothing out your short game.

Playing in Japan can be a thrill. You will never forget your golfing experience here. It will be as exciting as all the courses you will play, each one identifying with a different character. "Perfection" and "Pride" are dominant in these Japanese courses, and the "Love" they have for the game of golf is evident.

Other sporting facilities include 16 tennis courts, cycling paths, and swimming pools. As you can see, Karuizawa is a true golfing paradise. I have only one final suggestion: reserve some extra time to enjoy it all. YOU WILL LOVE IT.

An exclusive, world-famous resort in the Highlands area surrounded by great natural beauty.

"A trip to the heart of Japanese beauty"

Kawana Hotel

SHIZUOKA PREF., JAPAN

川奈ホテル

Your visit here will be a trip to the heart of Japanese beauty. From January to May, more than 4,000 trees of *sakura* (cherry blossoms) are in full bloom. Located in the suburbs of Ito City on Izu Peninsula, on a site overlooking the Pacific Ocean, Kawana offers a golfer immeasurable scenic delights.

The hotel was founded by the late Baron Kishichiro Okura, one of Japan's well-known businessmen, and a pioneer of tourism development.

Mr. Okura had a dream which has been fulfilled, that of making the Kawana Japan's first golf resort for foreigners. His name is synonymous with other hotel growth in Japan. Presently, there are 140 accommodations, modern and beautifully decorated. If you can visualize the surrounding beauty of the Izu-Hakone National Park, with towering Mount Fuji in the background, you will know you have been provided with a wealth of thrills.

You are in for a golfing experience as you take to the tee with its twists, obstacles, and a "full bag of tricks." The short (5,711 yards) Oshima course (named for the spectacular view of Oshima Island) was laid out by Mr. Komei Otani. Each hole is nicknamed; for example, #6 is "S.O.S.," a scenic ravine where shots are made across the deep valley. And "Good-Bye Hole" — #4 — is the perfect shot into the sea where many golfers have said "good-bye" to their balls — and maybe the game!

The Fuji course was designed by the British architect C.H. Allison, and plays 6,691 yards. This course demands considerable technique and skill. Of course Mount Fuji comes into play at all times — so keep your head down.

Besides the most picturesque environment Mother Nature can offer, you may enjoy swimming in one of their three pools, or playing tennis on the all-weather tennis courts.

The food at Kawana is as elegant as the surroundings. International foods are served and, of course, if you want delicate Japanese fare, this can be had in the quaint 350-year-old farm house that was transported from the mountains. The main dining room seats 50 people; the grill, 120. For tea and sweets, try the Sun Parlor, and at the "37th Hole" you will find a golfer's grill and bar.

A convention center was completed in 1978 and can accommodate up to 1,000 people.

You can reach the Kawana Hotel in two hours by express train from downtown Tokyo.

Golf here overlooks the Pacific Ocean, with Mt. Fuji always in play.

As you approach this beautifully situated resort 60 kilometers from Manila you will see clusters of rooms gracefully situated on hilly terrains. Across the coast line stretches the grand vista of Manila Bay at one end, and the Bataan peninsula on the other.

Room choices, include: Presidential suites, Executive suites, doubles, standards, moderate and superior.

Attractively decorated with every amenity including native interiors, set a relaxing mood.

The casual atmosphere, fine food and wine are winners here, and your food choices are varied...CAFE TERNATE serves Filipino and International cuisine in an exotic ethnic ambience.

La Parilla, a barbeque restaurant also offers International food, with continuous entertainment. NINI FRANCO features seafood and continental foods...Mardicas is open nightly and provides music for dancing and entertainment.

This 18 hole championship course is located a few blocks from the hotel, where you are provided with jeepney's, which are such fun, to take you about the property, and are available pronto...no waiting.

The Gary Player designed golf course is one of the most challenging you will ever play, and even some of your better shots will disappear from sight. A lot of hilly ups and downs, along with scenery so beautiful makes it hard to concentrate. A championship course consisting of 6,927 yards it is a par 72.

The imagination used here by Gary is overwhelming, you will feel a demand for accuracy.

A popular spot for major tournaments, they play hosts to many. Just when we decided this was a resort worthy of praise, we were then introduced to the sweetest nine-hole par three course, and I dare say there is not another one in the world that could surpass the fun or enjoyment of playing, and yet as challenging as you could find anywhere. The beauty is continuous, as each hole faces a different direction on the ocean. The rare beauty afforded you as you enjoy your favorite sport is truly a once in a life-time experience.

The Sports Pavilion, is a popular retreat among Presidents, Kings, and Movie Stars, plus spoiled golfing travelers. Here we found cottages authentically designed and decorated, plus being situated on the beach.

There is a lovely family styled restaurant, or you may have the service brought into your dining room, beautifully served.

Each cottage has a main house, with a combination living room and dining room and is exquistly decorated with all the comforts of home, your bedroom areas are separate.

Puerto Azul Beach Hotel Resort

PUERTO AZUL, PHILIPPINES

Continuous beauty, and rare finds have made this a popular retreat among Presidents, kings, stars and discerning travelers.

We found the food fabulous, and like the Filipinos we found hospitality #1. The health spa is located at the hotel poolside. There are swimming pools, tennis, water sports, beaching on a most beautiful and quiet beach, fishing, bowling and badminton, plus many wonderful trails for horseback riding, and squash.

If you need a tropical place for business they have a conference center, accommodating to 400 people.

If you are seeking the UNIQUE, quiet or active experience you cannot miss here.

The Rose Garden

NAKORN PATHOM, THAILAND

Occupying over 55 acres of former rice-fields, swamp and coconut orchards, the present-day Rose Garden Country Resort is a must to see.

In the early 1960's the present family owners supplied roses to Bangkok. Eventually, more and more people came to buy roses, and walk in the gardens. They began adding restaurants with Thai people in mind. Then the gardens were extended and more landscaping added until complete facilities were added and the Rose Garden Hotel opened in 1974, featuring first-class rooms, junior and deluxe suites, each with private balconies overlooking the River Nakorn Chaisri.

Not a large hotel by international standards, it is condusive to personal attention and service which they project in a warm family environment.

The rooms and suites are tastefully furnished, and extremely clean. The hotel is designed for informal convenience.

Apart from the hotel, with its elegant dining room, there is a poolside coffee shop, shopping arcade game rooms and a most fabulous Western bar done with the owners private antique collection. Additional antique Thai wooden houses offer an exciting change. They can get you in touch with Thai customs. They are located lakeside, also a motel with 14 more twin-bedded rooms is available.

There are excellent amenities for groups with fine conference facility selections.

For dining, a wide range is available apart from the hotel. The Chan Thai style restaurant or the floating Riverside Restaurant or perhaps the Ruen Pae Open Air Floating Restaurant for Chinese and Western food. Sala Loy features Thai food. Riverside Terrace is for lighter meals and they have a pianist at night, a cafeteria, plus numerous snack stalls. No one goes hungry here.

Truly a place to unwind and relax, it does exude a charm and comfort of yesteryear.

Known for the Thai Village Cultural Show, this spectacular showpiece of Thai life, culture, sport and pleasure will be a memory forever.

"There is always a "klong boy" on hand to dive in to rescue your submerged ball for a small fee."

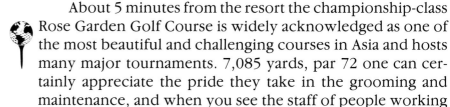

About 5 minutes from the resort the championship-class Rose Garden Golf Course is widely acknowledged as one of the most beautiful and challenging courses in Asia and hosts many major tournaments. 7,085 yards, par 72 one can certainly appreciate the pride they take in the grooming and maintenance, and when you see the staff of people working on it, it is obvious why it is so beautiful.

Aside from golf there are tennis courts, swimming pools, paddle and row boats, biking, horse and carriage rides and of course their trademark—"Elephant Rides." Don't miss this great experience.

Atlantik Beach Hotel

FREEPORT/LUCAYA, BAHAMAS

Located right by the world-renowned Lucaya Beach, the Atlantik Beach Hotel has 123 rooms and 52 split level quarters with living rooms. Almost ready after a complete renovation with special attention paid to every minute detail, this will be a four star deluxe hotel. Nothing has been spared. There are six European chefs in four restaurants to provide you with all the pleasures of the palate. All fronting spectacular views, even if you elect a casual evening, sumptuous buffets and menu ordering are served poolside.

The Lucayan Club has a luxurious clubhouse with a first-class restaurant offering a wide variety of specialties with sportsmen in mind. In the evening it is transformed into a gourmet restaurant, serving exotic dishes prepared by a French chef-de-cuisine.

The golf course is a golfer's paradise and is an 18-hole par 72. Designed by famed architect Dick Wilson, it is 6,824 yards long. The fairways are lined with pine trees and dense tropical underbrush, it is as pretty as it is challenging. The greens are elevated and are well bunkered. The Lucayan Country Club is owned by the hotel and though it is a short distance from the hotel, a regular scheduled bus service runs back and forth daily and complimentary. A well-stocked pro shop to serve you as well as putting greens, practice range etc.

Since the proprietors of the hotel are enthusiastic golfers, they know what the adherents of this sport are looking for. One of the most manicured courses you will play—always in superb condition.

Though the hotel has its own nightclub, you are only a five-minute taxi ride from the casino. Preparations are now being made to move the casino beachside adjacent to the hotel.

Of course, beachcombers love the clean, sandy beaches, snorkeling, water skiing, parachute flying, and many other facilities.

Since the hotel is Swiss-owned and managed, the mixture of European culture is readily felt. Yet the special flair of the Bahamas proves to be a successful combination.

Pine tree lined
fairways and dense
tropical
underbrush offers
each hole
seclusion.

Cotton Bay Club

ELUTHERA, BAHAMAS

A t this secluded hideaway you can find sand between your toes, a tropical drink in your hand, stars in your eyes, and a steward at your beck and call. At the Cotton Bay Club on Eluthera, one of the most attractive of the Bahamas' family islands, Nature has bestowed some serene beauty. A casual elegance permeates this deluxe resort as 77 white-roofed cottages nestle among the tall, graceful palms. The decor offers luxuriously comfortable rooms, which present all the comforts of home and then some! As you sip your cool drink on your private patio overlooking the sparkling ocean, you can sink into a state of relaxation that even you would not have felt was possible.

Cotton Bay Club was once the exclusive enclave of the very rich and the very powerful, and it is still fair to say that it is where "who's who in America goes barefoot in the Bahamas." However, Cotton Bay is open to anyone with an appreciation for privacy and simple elegance.

The food is artfully served with fascinating menus. A popular spot is the outdoor setup adjacent to the pool, where colorful linens and innovative table arrangements complement the stately surroundings. For intimate dining, the chef is noted for his Continental favorites as well as his Bohemian dishes.

"Where Who's Who in America goes barefoot in the Bahamas"

A deceptive challenge exists on the links because of tricky sea breezes; and you can be easily detracted by the sweeping vistas of azure sky, aquamarine water, and emerald grass. Imagine that chip shot to a green surrounded by ocean on three sides.

Continuing with your spirited play, if you need assistance, their friendly pro will give lessons. And Cotton Bay offers the only Robert Trent Jones golf course in the Bahamas.

Golf and tennis clinics are always "happening," plus bicycling, backgammon, shuffleboard and, of course, music and dancing under the stars after dinner.

Watersports? Try their marina: deep sea charters and SCUBA expeditions can be arranged.

A vacation at Cotton Bay can be as exciting as a wild ride on a windsurfer, or as relaxing as your day by the pool. Travel plans should be made well in advance from Miami. Remember: planes don't operate on a daily schedule.

Marriott's Castle Harbour Resort

TUCKER'S TOWN, BERMUDA

A classic Bermuda resort "now in the Marriott tradition."

One of Bermuda's classic resorts is now operating in the Marriott tradition. Nestled on a hilltop in the midst of 260 manicured subtropical acres, the property is surrounded by spectacular views of Castle Harbour and Harrington Sound.

A major restoration and expansion program featuring 120 new guest rooms, making a total of 415 rooms, new swimming pool and complete renovation of existing guest rooms is taking place at this writing. You can be sure particular emphasis will be placed on convenience, comfort as well as the best in decor. All feature panoramic views of the gardens, fairway and pools. Here old charm merges with modern conveniences.

Superb cuisine featuring Tepanyaki cooking and sushi in Mikado's, Bermuda's only Japanese restaurant. International cuisine is complemented by European service at the elegant Windsor Dining Room. Continental cuisine is offered at the Golf Club Restaurant, enhanced by views of the greens and Castle Harbour.

Music and ocean views accentuate tea service and cocktails at the Bayview lounge afternoons. Sip your favorite drink at Blossom's, a Japanese-style lounge. Always a hit!!! The Golf Club Bar near the 1st tee is popular with all.

Speaking of golf—the par 71 18-hole championship golf course designed by Robert Trent Jones has an international reputation and has hosted many famous tournaments. Known not only for its beauty among the pros and guests, it is challenging as well—a dramatic course, with undulating fairways. Though it is not a long course there are plenty of hazards to affect your shots if you are not in the fairway.

A clubhouse, and pro shop as well as the Golf Club Restaurant enhance your golfing stay here.

Three swimming pools, one with a beautiful waterfall, plus crystalline beaches are other sporting options.

Tennis with nightlighted courts are yours to enjoy, too. Complete conference facilities with excellent outdoor facilities lend themselves to extravagant pool parties, barbecues and receptions of up to 1,000 guests.

Castle Harbour, Bermuda's classic resort is nestled on a hilltop in the midst of 260 manicured subtropical acres, surrounded by spectacular views of Castle Harbour and Harrington Sound.

Banff Springs Hotel

BANFF, ALBERTA, CANADA

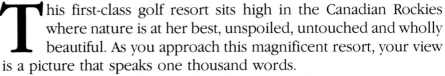

*"Sitting
one mile high,
where nature
is at her
best"*

This first-class golf resort sits high in the Canadian Rockies where nature is at her best, unspoiled, untouched and wholly beautiful. As you approach this magnificent resort, your view is a picture that speaks one thousand words.

You are assured a comfortable stay in the newly renovated rooms, which are available in single rooms with a parlor, executive suites, or split level suites.

For your dining pleasures there are a variety of fine restaurants. The Main Dining Room is a most popular spot because of its varietal menu and consistently good food. The Expresso Cafe with an extensive menu adds a special touch to any day or evening. If you are in the mood for French cuisine the Rob Roy is a perfect spot where all food is served in the European manner. Another choice is the beautiful Alhambra Room where the menu changes daily and buffets are the highlight. If you are craving something on the light side, undoubtedly the Pot Pourri will fill your bill. If you enjoy a dance during dinner, the Alberta Room offers a pleasant evening. It is easy to see why vacationers choose Banff for their golf get aways as there is such varied opportunity.

Golfing at Banff is a special experience and the elaborate scenery is mind-boggling. When this golf course which sits one mile high was designed, an estimated $500,000 was spent on it. At today's costs, it would exceed $4 million.

While we played this impressive course, full-grown deer and baby bear cubs scurried out in front of our golf shots. Since Banff National Park is a game reserve, the animals are fearless and, generally, quite tame, so you see you need not worry…

The championship course is very picturesque and the 6,729-yard 18 holes offer a golfing challenge you may never forget. Deadly accuracy is called for due to the well-placed traps. Skillfully designed by Stanley Thompson, the course has one of the best reputations, not only among amateurs and travelers, but among professionals as well.

Since this has been the home of many tournaments, Banff may not need a formal introduction; once you experience all the Banff Resort has to offer, you will cherish special memories.

Gray Rocks

ST. JOVITE,
QUEBEC, CANADA

G ray Rocks Inn — the dean of the Laurentian Mountains — is an enchanting course in spring, summer, and autumn. It is situated on the crystal-clear waters of Lac Ouimet in a relaxing, unhurried atmosphere where you can collect your thoughts for that hole-in-one.

Many accommodations are available, depending on your preference. You may choose a quaint room in their main lodge or a deluxe chalet *Swisse,* where you can enjoy a private balcony overlooking the lake. Roomy log cabins are also available and, just a short distance from the Inn, Le Chateau exudes a European flavor. Whatever your choice, you are certain to enjoy perfect comfort.

Dining is sumptuous with breakfast, lunch, and dinner each

presenting a new experience. The many specialties of the house will please your most demanding tastes. Try to diet, if necessary, before you go because you're guaranteed to gain a pound or two.

After dinner, there is still plenty of fun to be had, whether it be a bonfire on the beach, or dancing to Gray Rocks' swingin' combo.

Lac Ouimet's crystal clear water reflects the relaxed, unhurried atmosphere of Gray Rocks.

 An extremely interesting 18-hole layout, Par 72, will test your skills, and the golf course is surrounded by mountains, fresh air, trees, and sparkling lakes.

One unusual hole, #14, a Par 3, 160 yards for men, has no fairway and is on a steep hill with a very small green. You can make a two here or a seven as easily. For ladies it is only 125 yards, but still requires a perfect shot.

If you can stand all this natural beauty, and still keep your head down, you are apt to play a memorable game.

With your choice of fun and games to fill the day, there is never a dull moment. Tennis can be played on 22 fast-drying Hartru courts; or try your luck at lawn bowling, volleyball, boating, and water skiing. Sunbathing on Gray Rocks' beautiful sandy beach — along with delectable food service and other amenities — will leave you with a good taste in your mouth.

Besides the summer fun, Gray Rocks is a world famous ski resort.

"The Dean of the Laurentian Mountains"

Jasper Lodge

JASPER, ALBERTA, CANADA

Clear water of Lac Beauvert, above, reflects majestic mountains in Jasper National Park, a serene and lovely setting for a sensational golfing experience.

Jasper Lodge is surrounded by the majestic mountains and accented by the stately pines of Canada's Jasper National Park. One of the most scenic and picturesque settings you will ever see is the mirrored clear water of Lac Beauvert which sparkles with just a hint of jade blue.

The Lodge at Jasper consists of 54 chalets plus the main building, able to accommodate more than 700 guests. Not content to rest on their laurels, the staff at Jasper are constantly refurbishing and updating to assure their guests of the very best.

It is obvious why they display their Five Diamond Award proudly, a distinct honor awarded by the American and Canadian Automobile Associations. Only eight other hotels in Canada share this honor.

Rooms and suites are joined by pathways and include the new Deluxe Beauvert Suites, feature sitting rooms, living rooms, dining rooms, patios, and log-burning fireplaces. The decor is charming and you feel immediately at home as you sit enjoying the fireplace.

Combining the joys of the outdoors with the comfort and convenience of the indoors is what I remember most. We never will forget the beautiful deer that were so tame; they would just as soon keep you company while you are teeing up. While we were driving to this lovely resort, we saw the Jasper bears; of course, we were smart enough to roll our windows up. They're very curious.

The most sensational thing I remember about the golf was how well manicured everything was. Certainly the next thing was the challenge. This is the home of many professional tournaments, and I understand that the Seniors will be playing there again in 1983.

Mostly, the challenge is in keeping your head down. With such natural, magnificent beauty everywhere including the snow-tipped mountains, lakes, flowers, and trees, you must concentrate.

The fourth hole is one of the prettiest, but with a hogback green and lots of water to go over, I can't say it was my favorite. Number 15 is "Bad Baby," rightly named even though it is the shortest hole. It is full of heartache. Championship tees play 6,590 yards and Par 71.

Aside from the scenery and great golf, the service and the food are excellent. Four main dining rooms are available to satisfy any palate. When the sun goes down, there is always live entertainment and dancing, plus quiet relaxation in the lounge.

Other favorite pastimes are bicycling, canoeing, rafting, or shopping in the quaint town of Jasper. Take the sky tram. Tennis (lots of it), paddleboatings, jogging, or wandering through the trails are all good ways to spend your time. Maybe you could have your picture taken with "Jasper the Bear" in the train station. Ride the horse that Paul Newman rode in the movie *Prime Cut;* Scout is now a resident of the Jasper Park Lodge Riding Academy. Welcome to Jasper!

"Combining the joys of the outdoors with the comforts and conveniences of the indoors"

Britannia

GRAND CAYMAN, BRITISH WEST INDIES

*The first golf
course in
the Caymans—
"The first course to
use the Cayman
ball".*

B ritannia is a golf course community, being designed and built to reflect a casual elegance in lifestyle on the Caribbean Island of Grand Cayman, British West Indies.

At this writing Hyatt is building a 240 room luxury hotel in the typical Hyatt tradition. When completed there will also be 400 condominium residences.

Situated 480 miles due south of Miami and 180 miles west of Jamaica there are 18,000 English speaking residents.

This 88-acre Britannia development is located across from the world-famous Seven Mile Beach.

The golf course has been completed and is open for play, and was designed by Jack Nicklaus and his associates.

The course includes a 9-hole regulation length layout, and 18-hole executive course, and an 18-hole Cayman Ball course, all combined into one.

The 9-hole measures 3,180 yards and plays to a par 35, or if the Cayman ball is used it becomes an 18-hole course. Simply put, the ball will allow players to play a regulation game of golf, with the ball going half the distance on each shot...Some controversy surrounds this, but you will have to admit "THIS IS UNIQUE".

They have created a look and feel of a Scottish course, with water, oversized bunkers, blind tee shots, grassy mounds and rolling dunes.

On #5 water comes into play three times...

The Cayman Ball course is the first in the world to utilize the Cayman Ball developed by Jack Nicklaus and his Mac Gregor Golf Company, and is one of the newest innovations in recent golf history.

When completed also in the plan are a number of tennis courts, plus a full service marina accommodating all sizes of sportscraft and yachts. Add fishing, surfing, windsailing, water and jet skiing and you get the sports resort picture here. Britannia Beach Club with all facilities when completed is adjacent to the property.

The location offers privacy and seclusion, tranquil waterways, Caribbean breezes, and definitely the rythms of life are more gentle; however if you tire of solitude, peace and tranquility you may opt for shopping at their duty free port, promising the best shopping and bargains to be found anywhere.

Casa De Campo

LA ROMANA,
DOMINICAN REPUBLIC

I f you have dreamed of a true tropical paradise, your dream will come true at the Grand Hotel at Casa de Campo. It is operated by Gulf & Western, and offers the finest in accommodations, golf, and casual or fine dining.

As you arrive at this 7,000-acre Dominican estate, a montage of some of the world's most breathtaking scenery surrounds you. You may opt to stay in the main hotel, the casitas, or in the villas, all of which have been decorated by native son Oscar de la Renta. The design is innovative and typical of the country; it reflects elegance.

Two championship golf courses challenge you. "Teeth of the Dog" is laid out along the coast, lined with beautiful jade green water and reefs. Inland, the countryside provides a backdrop. Playing here is similar to playing at Pebble Beach where miles and miles of shoreline make it difficult to concentrate. But take your eye off the ball at your own risk.

Take note of hole #7, which incidentally happened to be my favorite, not only because of the challenge but because of its

grandeur as well. One finds it hard to believe that this is a Par 3, as it measures 179 yards and is totally surrounded by ocean. The course itself runs 6,787 yards from the regular tees, but it is no easy number.

The second course, the Links, is an inland course reminiscent of famous Scottish courses. It measures 6,327 yards from the championship tee. Both courses were designed by the renowned architect, Peter Dye.

Dining options are from the casual to the very elegant, to satisfy most moods. For breakfast or lunch, you may choose the El Lago Grill which overlooks the 18th hole at the "Teeth of the Dog." You'll enjoy the quiet that seems to result when Caribbean waters dominate any scene.

If it is a very special dining experience you are looking for, try the famed Tropicana, which features Dominican and international specialties. Candlelight and music complement any dish you may choose.

La Piazetta at Altos de Chavon offers superb Italian food in a country inn atmosphere. Les Canaris is an elegant country French restaurant catering to the discriminating gourmet. It is open for dinner only. At Las Minitas Beach, beach parties and folk shows provide a diversion from more traditional meals. Varied menus include selections of French, Italian, Dominican, Chinese, and special seafoods.

The area also has a unique re-creation of a 16th Century artisan's village at Altos de Chavon. It is just minutes from Casa de Campo, but still on the same property. The project was begun to support the area's international painters, sculptors, artists, and weavers. It's quite a change of pace and a "must" to visit. You can stay at a quaint hotel on the property for a taste of 16th Century living.

Emerging as a superstar in other sports, the Casa offers many side surprises in their marina such as snorkeling, deep sea fishing, sailing, and skin diving.

There are five swimming pools, numerous tennis complexes, and a polo club. Incidentally, this is one of the few international resort polo teams in the world. Skeet and trap shooting also are available.

Regularly scheduled carriers fly into the Santo Domingo airport every day from New York, Miami, Detroit, San Juan, Caracas and Madrid. You may rent a car there, and the drive to the hotel will take approximately two hours.

On advance reservation, transportation is available from the Las Americas Airport. If you prefer, the hotel's 6,200-foot private airstrip can accommodate you.

Keep in mind that U.S. citizens will need a tourist card, birth certificate, or passport.

The climate is mild, with average temperatures of 70°F in the winter and 80°F in the summer. Dress is casual, ties and jackets optional, and light sweaters are recommended.

Achieving harmony by taking advantage of the magnificent oceanfront, Cerromar Beach Hotel is eight stories tall with a double-Y configuration. It is a visual delight, as you watch the curving beach on one side and the rolling hills of Puerto Rico in the distance.

This beautiful estate was once a densely foliaged swamp alongside a windswept, barren wasteland. The transformation that has been achieved is indescribable, pure pleasure to see. It was hard to realize that such an accomplishment could have been possible. From the moment you arrive at this luxurious hotel you will be stimulated by all the creating that has taken place.

A gemlike hotel welcomes you, approached by winding, palm-lined driveways and a bridge spanning reflecting pools. The Cerromar's open air design incorporates the outside in a graceful and flowing manner. This beautiful spread is universally recognized as a premier resort, and I certainly found nothing lacking. The Cerromar Beach Hotel is definitely a horticultural showplace with a staff of 40 fulltime gardeners.

The hotel has 508 rooms, all air conditioned for your comfort and offering your choice of rooms or suites.

 Two superb golf courses designed by Robert Trent Jones will require a cohesive effort on any golfer's part and can be surprisingly "consuming" if you give them a chance.

The dramatically situated 7th hole was my favorite, and it probably will be yours. The ocean rolling right at its side resembles a looking glass. This hole is truly a creation of mood and atmosphere.

A unique offering at this beautiful resort is that with Dorado Beach as Cerromar Beach's sister hotel, any guest at either hotel may play as much golf as he or she desires, with a choice of four courses.

Cerromar Beach Hotel

DORADO BEACH,
PUERTO RICO

Come evening, Club Cerromar is on stage, as are the gracious meals so appetite-appealing that your imagination will be entertained by the chef's originality. Having a kitchen that a chef dreams of, their chef had a direct voice in design and selection of equipment. Can you feel his important role already? Precious china and traditional settings, along with colorful lavishness in flowers, are just a few of the amenities dominating a romantic evening.

Their famous Surf Room features elegant oceanview dining. The Garden Room is a delight, serving sumptuous breakfasts and lunches fit for a king or queen — and for you! With a plentiful supply of fresh fish and fruits, they offer mouthwatering and tempting dishes.

El Bucanero Restaurant for your lighter moods offers informal *a la carte* menus. El Coqui Club is a very fine bar and offers dancing nightly, but it is so comfortably appointed that you may prefer to sit back and just "people watch."

El Yunque Lounge, a little greenhouse, looks like a glassed-in jungle, always offering perfect drink pacifiers and a bit of music. The Beach Bohio Bar is located between the beach and the bar in a relaxing tropical setting. Finally, the Golf Clubhouse is available for snacks or an informal lunch.

Exercise classes are held daily at Cerromar Beach, and they have an archery range, along with tennis, bicycling, sailboating, and sunbathing.

If your tolerance level is seeking tradewinds and a tropical climate of approximately 79 degrees year-round, then you'd better slip on that jet and enjoy...

"Pure pleasure to see"

Two Robert Trent Jones-designed courses await the traveling golfer at Cerromar with more golf available at nearby Dorado Beach.

The individualistic and relaxing Dorado Beach Hotel provides a spectacular setting for broadening your horizons in fine dining and golf. You are guaranteed that quality predominates here. Laurance Rockefeller, who originated Dorado Beach in grand manner, stated, "In building our resort, we go to the frontiers of natural beauty and keep them in harmony with the locale."

Formerly a grapefruit and coconut plantation, the hotel was opened with 136 rooms in 1958. Today, they boast 300 rooms spread out in different locales on the property. Dorado Beach is richly garnished with native trees, flowing contours, and abundant native flowering delights.

Because of the expansive area, and with the accommodations scattered about, you enter into a serene and unhurried love affair with a mystic environment.

You have two world famous Robert Trent Jones golf courses to choose from, each distinctive from the other. Both courses challenge the expert but give the weekend golfer a sporting chance. The layout is noted for its lakes, the sparkling sea, and a rich atmosphere of palm trees. The fairways on both the East Course and the West Course are beautifully laid out and will offer you a substantial challenge.

Under the experienced management of Regent International Hotels, the Dorado Beach is known for paying attention to every detail. They maintain Old World standards of service for all their guests, and when you enter this hotel, you enter a different world, a timeless style that is very personal. It has been said that Dorado is a "jewel" surrounded by the natural charms of Puerto Rico.

Superb dining is a legend at Su Casa. Smooth service, stylized bouquets, flickering candlelight, charm and elegance plus subtle glamour enhance a worthy evening. Su Casa boasts the distinction of having served many world dignitaries. The melodic sounds of *Los Tunates,* a five gentlemen musical group, can be heard each evening as they delight guests while strolling through the restaurant. A great deal of care has been taken in restoring and maintaining the Spanish atmosphere of Su Casa. It is a personal experience that exemplifies the restaurant's motto: "My house is yours."

Palate testing may also be enjoyed at the Surf and Galley Rooms. Continental dishes are served in the three-tiered Surf Room, overlooking the breaking surf. Spontaneous and sure, the Ocean Terrace awaits its guests, serving breakfast and lunch on an open terrace. A perfect spot for a light snack is available at the first tees of the two 18-hole courses.

Puerto Rico is a naturally air-conditioned island with a benevolent climate year-round, averaging 79 degrees. Daily jet service is available from major cities to San Juan International Airport, and guests may be ticketed from there through Dorado Beach Airport via Crownair. Limousine service will be furnished on request.

Dorado Beach Hotel

DORADO BEACH, PUERTO RICO

Home of Chi Chi Rodriguez, who feels that the 13th hole at Dorado is the most challenging he has played.

"The Jewel of the Caribbean"

Mahogany Run

ocated just minutes from Magen Bay on the beautiful island of St. Thomas, Mahogany Run is becoming one of the most sought-after golf resorts in the Caribbean. It is only 10 minutes from Charlotte Amalie, the capital city of the Virgin Islands, and 15 minutes from Truman International Airport.

As you motor in by car, bus, or limousine, you will notice that the roads wind around some of the most spectacular routes you have ever seen. I can recall the last curve in the road before approaching the resort as such a lush display of nature's majesty that I almost had to pinch myself. I couldn't believe it was so beautiful. Rich vibrant colors, mountain breezes plus the exotic and sensual Caribbean certainly heightened my already brimming enthusiasm.

George and Tom Fazio are responsible for this delightful, but tough, golf course. When you finish here, you know that you have had a true test of your skill. The mountain pass is so tight, you more than likely will use your irons frequently; we did. And the heavy foliage will make you keep your head down, if nothing else will.

It has been said that the storied course rises and falls like a roller coaster, especially on its journey by the sea. The 13th, 14th, and 15th holes make up "the Devil's Triangle," and that's no joke. Plan to have a lot of balls for it is not uncommon to hit the best shot you ever had, straight down the middle, and never find it. It seems the devil just carries it away.

Mahogany Run

ST. THOMAS, U.S. VIRGIN ISLANDS

The basic criterion for the design of the course was to have a place that would have outstanding character for both member and resort play. My honest opinion is that it has real character, all right! If I could keep reliving my most memorable golf holes forever, I would have to say that there is no more spectacular hole in the world than Number 13. This is the one you see in most magazines. There is trouble for the best golfer in front.

Though this resort is fairly new, predictions are that it is on its way to fame. At this writing, 50 more rooms are being added which will bring the total up to 175.

Besides being a golfer's paradise, there are also plenty of things for the non-golfer to do. A new tennis village is being built, along with another swimming pool and a health spa. You may choose snorkeling along the coral reefs, sailing down through Drakes Bay or going deep sea fishing. If you can stand to miss a day of golf, do try the shopping in St. Thomas: the best shopping almost in the world.

Your personal accommodations are brightly colored and well-decorated. All rooms have stunning views, plus many have their own private pool. Because the hotel has its own nursery, you will be impressed with the lavish landscaping, dominated by colorful flowers and tropical plants.

Dining is less casual, but there's nothing casual about the food. The culinary variations are exquisite.

"A lush display of nature's majesty"

Tryall

HANOVER, JAMAICA

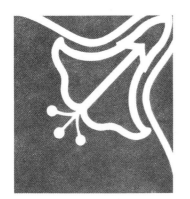

Unparalleled beauty emanates from this surprising luxury hotel located on the Island of Jamaica's northern coast, approximately 12 miles west of Montego Bay. Situated on a 2,200-acre plantation which has been owned by a private family for more than a century, it is superb.

The accent here is on each guest's comfort and convenience. When we arrived a day earlier than scheduled (a teeny mistake I made), it was obvious to me that they were much more upset than I since they had no extra rooms.

Resorts Management, Inc., is improving this resort all the time. The rooms are very comfortable and private. Maids around every corner make sure you have brightly colored fresh flowers and immaculate surroundings at all times. The great house hotel is a genuine reflection of historic days in true "Jamaican style."

Besides the hotel, there is an offering of individual cottages staffed with your own private cook, housemaid, laundress, and gardener and featuring your own private swimming pool.

If you like romantic hideaways, this is a must. Adorning the dining room at the great house are soft pink linen cloths with bright fresh native flowers, both inviting and enjoyable.

You are served, unpretentiously, the finest gourmet food available. We were simply astounded when we discovered that they made their own sweet butter, churned their own ice cream, and, if that was not enough, we sampled a bite of English toffee made on the spot in their own kitchen.

By this time, we were raving since it had been one of those days you dream about; then the night's entertainment was underway. The resident orchestra had all of us on our feet until the wee hours.

From the main dining room, you have a sweeping view of the bay plus the sparkling pool with its waterfall adding beauty to your stay.

Quiet hospitality and friendly, gracious service make Tryall a perfect place for a Jamaican holiday.

At the Golf and Beach Club is a casual dining area which also has a special view overlooking the bay, offering special drinks and food to go with it.

 A Par 71 course winds gracefully through coconut and palm trees, wandering from inland to seaside spots and back again. Ponds, wild birds, and natural foliage in variations are everywhere.

Most tropical courses need to be played in the morning, but not so at Tryall. Mornings are on the muggy side; we found that afternoons offered the gentle breezes from the Cockpit Mountains. Mornings were good for relaxing, bicycling, horseback riding, or tennis. Golf at this 18-hole championship course has become international and certainly is the finest in Jamaica. Your caddies are such fun and really put themselves out for the guests of Tryall.

"The accent is on comfort and convenience"

When making travel arrangements for this spectacular resort, remember to bring your passport even if it has expired. Plan ahead for ground transportation, as hustling seemed to be the name of the game at the airport. Since our plane was late, and we arrived at midnight, it was an experience I wouldn't want to repeat again.

Rising from the lapping waters of Ireland's second biggest lake, Lough Corrib with its 365 islands, Ashford Castle has stood sentinel over Irish affairs since its birth in 1228. The story of Ashford itself is the history of Ireland. Reaching back into antiquity, it reflects the character of the country and its people.

It has been said Ashford and its quaint old adjoining village of Cong encompass all that is best in Irish life.

The setting is like a picture postcard countryside, touched and nurtured by the azure beauty, indeed a romantic setting in a serene land. The stark yet attractive outline almost merges with the scenery.

Built over a period of 30 years by Lord Ardiluan in the 19th Century, the resort still incorporates the remains of a 13th Century de Burgo Castle and the original Ashford House built in the style of a French chateau. In more recent years, it has been renovated and luxuriously appointed to create one of Europe's premier castles. Beautifully crafted furnishings, paintings by celebrated artists, and other *objets d'art* recall the elegance and creativity of the past. Guest rooms number 79.

Each room is different, many being suites. The decor handsomely complements the overall scene. The elegance and dignity of style are in the traditional manner but with today's comforts.

Their food is prepared and served with admirable integrity and taste. Each meal is presented with flair and their professional skill is everywhere in evidence. You may enjoy a thirst quencher in the Corrib Lounge or the River Lounge, but wherever, you can be assured a priceless time and curiously when you leave, the memories you take home will be timeless and tranquil.

As you approach the 9-hole golf course, bewitching sights abound. The wide lawns are alive with floral color and graceful flowing fountains. A silhouette of distant hills spread out beautifully. The almost perfectly manicured fairways are among formal gardens. Catching a glimpse of the great cut-stone bridge over the lake, you can transport yourself for one of the most serene and peaceful courses you will ever play.

The legendary beauty of the golf at Ashford makes this still another place where you would wish time to stand still. Each shot is placed in an almost unforgettable atmosphere. The course is maintained exclusively for the enjoyment of the guests. It is not particularly hard, but tricky and very enjoyable. Have you ever hit your ball from a shamrock-shaped trap? You will here. Who knows? Should you hit your ball in there, you may have the luck of the Irish getting out.

Ashford Castle

ASHFORD, IRELAND

"The story of Ashford is the history of Ireland"

Numerous flower gardens are yours to explore, and if that is not enough, you may choose to play tennis, take a boat ride, go on a picnic, or just relax.

A favorite place of dignitaries, presidents, and notables from all over the world, Ashford Castle will probably be yours, too.

Situated in the heart of Central Switzerland, atop a mountain peninsula, Bürgenstock is 3,000 feet above sea level and 1,500 feet above Lake Lucerne. The entire mountain is covered with forests and fields, and to walk through this place of unspoiled scenery is a tremendous experience.

There are three hotels — the Grand Hotel, the Palace Hotel, and the Park Hotel — each decorated to identify with its name and a most enjoyable sight to behold. The hotels are accented with fabulous antiques and priceless paintings by many world-renowned artists, so make it a point to enjoy *objets d'art* in your leisure time.

Beautiful fresh flower arrangements everywhere add extra beauty, and all flowers are raised in their own greenhouses.

The philosophy of this resort is to foster enterprise on the mountain through aesthetics, culture, and hospitality, and to express them all in a unique synthesis. The resort's history dates back to 1872 when the Grand Hotel opened. The Park Hotel opened in 1888 and the Palace Hotel, in 1904.

Guests may choose between the three, and it can be difficult. Each room is different and decorated comfortably with all modern conveniences.

Many restaurants offer Swiss and Italian specialties in atmospheres from the rustic Tavern to the Zur Trotte, with varying price ranges. Of course, the formal dining rooms serving continental cuisine are a grand event at any of the three hotels.

The informal Lakeside Inn Kehrsiten is a must to see. You will ride the Bürgenstock funicular to the shore of Lake Lucerne. This is a cozy place for a snack and some commanding views.

The Bürgenstock Estate

BÜRGENSTOCK, SWITZERLAND

 The nine-hole golf course is unreal. If you were a mountain goat, it could help, maybe…A combination of the greatest golf architects could not come up with more interest and excitement.

Be aware there are no electric carts, and golfing here can be trying, but once you acclimate yourself, it can be some of the greatest fun you could have on any course.

If you can tune into a cowbell symphony, this is what is in store for you: The fairways are strewn with miniature wild flowers in various colors, while still being well groomed. Greens are carefully tended, and though there's not much water, traps play an integral part on your score card.

The layout of this course, along with some of the world's most beautiful scenery, cannot be beat, especially if you want peace, quiet, and serenity.

Wait until you see the pro shop. It is marvelously quaint, as is the clubhouse itself.

If you can imagine a typical resort in Switzerland, you have it here. Swimming, hiking, sightseeing, nature walks, and shopping in their fine shops are fun to incorporate for a perfect holiday.

"Aesthetics, culture, and hospitality"

The Belfry

WISHAW, NORTH WARWICKSHIRE, ENGLAND

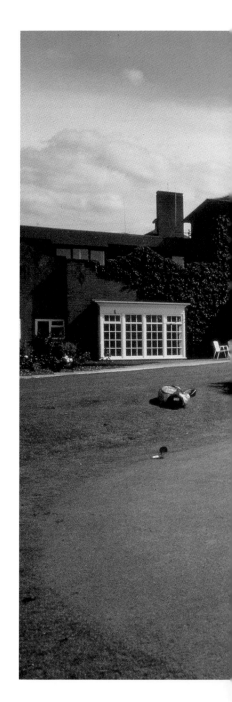

In a class of its own, The Belfry stands amidst 360 acres of beautiful parkland.

One hundred and sixty five bedrooms are luxurious and a pleasure to occupy. Decorated in a traditional manner or modern they afford you a choice of high standards.

The Belfry, an oasis of calm, is close to Britain's second city, and is surrounded by many things to do and see, including some of Britain's finest castles and stately homes.

The Belfry's award winning French restaurant is sure to win your approval, as well as the "Buttery Grill" for your favorite drink, or a quiet cozy atmosphere. The Chalet Pub is located in a park, and of course the Spike Bar is always enjoyable while swapping golf stories.

Speaking of golf, you have two truly great golf courses. The Derby is extremely exciting measuring 6,077 yards, it is a par 70. The Brabazon makes The Belfry a mecca for golfers from all over the world, and is Venue for the 1985 Ryder Cup. The Belfry's Brabazon course has been host for Lawrence Batley International Tournament, the State Express Classic and the Hennessy Cognac Cup.

Many of the worlds leading players have played this most exciting course and many stake claims that it is their favorite. Designed by Peter Alliss and Dave Thomas, they are both challenging, but a handicap of 28 or less is required to enjoy the Brabazon.

The quality of the golf is matched by the quality of the hotel itself. It is truly one of Britains finest hotels and is enhanced by a quiet professionalism that you can count on.

If you are inclined for a round of tennis, squash, swimming, or a wonderful spa experience, they are all here.

"Your golf at The Belfry can be an experience you won't want to miss."

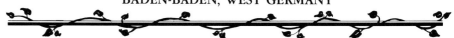

Brenner's Park-Hotel

BADEN-BADEN, WEST GERMANY

*The glorious experience
of outrageous luxury can be
yours forever...*

If you want outrageous luxury and a holiday in Europe's fabled spa city, this glorious experience can be yours for a price. At the moment you arrive, a green-aproned porter will appear to assist with your luggage, someone else will spin the revolving door, and the concierge will welcome you by name. Brenner has a magical formula for keeping its hotel really *tout grand*.

You will be escorted immediately to your room while being informed about the foreign rate of exchange and tipping. Great effort by the staff ensures that you feel "at home." And if you are impressed by beautiful things, you will enjoy the Brenner's Park-Hotel with all five senses.

Spacious accommodations with every amenity blend modern comforts and sedate period furniture, portraying a feeling of long-standing tradition. Fine linens, down pillows, and comforters are just a few special items.

When the maid turns the bed down, she places your slippers on a clean towel laid on the rug. Appropriate hangers for skirts, pants, etc., plus clothes trees in the bedroom, are an added convenience and consideration. In the large marble bath, you will find warm towels on your heated rack. Masses of linens, Rochas soap, bath scales, magnifying mirrors, bath thermometers and, last but not least, elegant perfumes contribute to a great stay. If you have room service, a lovely rose will brighten up the serving cart, while a pantry on every floor expedites your food service, and your food does arrive good and hot.

Can you imagine 220 servants for 200 beds? Almost a host per guest. A book could be written on the service alone. Such care is a relic of bygone days, which has somehow managed to survive the industrial era here.

The Brenner has a personal card on file for all their guests, describing what kind of mattress you prefer, what type pillow, what kind of champagne, furniture, etc. Rooms are always decorated with fresh flowers.

Don't miss lunch and gourmet dining in the Schwarzwald Grill. The cuisine at Brenner's Park-Hotel is excellent, prepared under the direction of head chef, Albert Keelner.

The grounds are park-like with majestic oaks sprawled everywhere. Add tulip trees, azaleas, rose beds, and hedges, and strolling becomes a pleasure. The hotel is located on the banks of the gentle Oos and is stocked with lively trout.

A beautiful 18-hole golf course provides a challenge and great interest, tempting you to be on the course continuously. We could never play enough golf here. We found it hard to play while taking in all the beauty of flowers, perfectly groomed fairways, and lovely greens. Though this is a private course, guests of the Brenner's Park-Hotel are welcomed.

The course is not particularly hard, but is particularly enjoyable. The backdrop of pine-covered mountains adds to the beauty.

The daily routine at Brenner's resembles shipboard life: sports clothes and comfortable walking shoes for daytime activities; for evening chic, suits or dresses are the rule. What fun checking out the beautiful wardrobes and jewelry!

Ah yes, their world renowned spa — with the cell therapy — is located in the Villa Stephanie where Napoleon III once lived.

Now big news! The Lancaster Beauty Farm is a must for women and men. The "Farm" includes skin and body care, yoga, massage, and dieting.

Tennis and gambling, plus the wonderful golf, are quite a performance from a hotel resort. Among the luxury hotels of Europe — jewels whose fire is fading — this cultivated former sanatorium remains a fine polished diamond.

"A fine polished diamond"

Dona Filipa Hotel

ALGARVE, PORTUGAL

"A Paradise Found"

*With the most picturesque
setting and visual beauty,
Dona Filipa offers the utmost
in luxury and service.*

In an ideal setting among fig, almond, and pine trees, this is a five-star luxury hotel that lives up to them. When we were their guests, we knew it! Service is first and foremost to this award-winning resort, and though we were a long way from home, we felt extremely comfortable. The hospitality and the service are the features that will linger in your mind.

Remembering the accommodations that consisted of either a beautiful, spacious, and well decorated room at the hotel or a carefully designed villa or apartment still reminds me of something special. All offer a superb setting with the amenities you would expect, and some you may not. Most of the villas, and apartments as well, have their own gardens and swimming pools!

Throughout the complex, you are provided with free transportation to any sport you wish to participate in. However, the golf course is very easily reached.

"Five stars and she lives up to them"

 The Vale do Lobo Golf Club has 27 holes, broken up and named by colors. Playing the Red Course, you will have a spectacular view of the ocean on many holes, and as a matter of fact, you will be playing along the beach most of the time. As I reminisce about the beaches in Portugal, what I remember is miles and miles without a footprint, so perfect that you feel no one else knows it exists.

The Yellow Course has become famous because of its #7 hole. Many golfers all over the world identify with this popular hole. From tee to green, it has a lot of carry over the sandstone cliffs and is almost impossible, a 200-yard Par 3.

The Green Course is the most recent, but is firmly established in the golf trio. The general condition of these holes surpasses anything in Portugal, and this is precisely why it is a must course on any traveling golfer's itinerary. All three courses are considered luxury, and when we were there, everything was lush and green.

Dona Filipa is frequented by the local trade, because their food has a reputation as some of the finest on the Algarve. Not only is the atmosphere friendly and the food delicious, but the menu has so many choices!

If you enjoy a restaurant overlooking a beautiful swimming pool, you will choose the Rotunda, offering a good international menu. The Prata ("square") is filled with charm and a choice of Bistro pizzeria, Faro cafeteria, and the Vivant cocktail bar. For the night person, the Kasbah nightclub may be exciting and offers disco, too.

Next time we have a chance to travel in this area, you can be sure we'll visit this beautiful spot again.

Dolder Grand

ZURICH, SWITZERLAND

This is a prominent landmark of Zurich, ranked number four on the list of the world's best hotels. Stately, it stands as a most unique turn-of-the-century example of architecture. It combines traditional and contemporary, up-to-date facilities. We were so impressed with our first visit that we have recommended it to our good travelling friends.

The 198-room hostelry overlooking Lake Zurich has a commanding view with the Alps as a backdrop.

How long has it been since you have had fresh-cut flowers delivered to your room each day? Pressing done overnight? Timely wake-up calls? Even the quality of the creme they use to polish your shoes is chosen with care.

A fun feature is the Dolder funicular which leaves for the city every 10 minutes. It is free for Dolder Grand guests.

The resort is approximately six minutes from the center of town and 20 minutes from the airport.

Besides the traditional rooms with every amenity one would expect, there are Junior suites and Grand suites with views of the lake, the Alps, and the city, plus a few overlooking the forest park.

For your dining pleasures, restaurant La Rotonde features exquisite French cuisine, formal in the evenings, and sweeping views of the mountains and the golf course.

An open-air terrace for dining opened during the season. A bar and lounge with a piano and tea is available in the lobby every afternoon.

Extensive woods, for walking or jogging, and tennis courts are free for guests; as are the nine holes of golf.

Ranked number four on the list of the world's best hotels.

"Traditional and contemporary combined"

Somewhere, sometime, a world-class golfer may only have time for nine holes, and because of my fondness for this very special place I felt sharing nine holes would be welcomed. But if you choose more, you can always play twice!

Dromoland Castle

NEWMARKET ON FERGUS, COUNTY CLARE, IRELAND

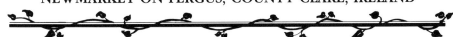

T he Ireland of a thousand romantic yesterdays is a perfect setting for a golfing holiday, and a perfect spot for a nine-hole warmup while getting over your jet lag. Dromoland Castle can be your answer.

When you arrive at this now magnificent resort hotel, the fairytale setting reminds you of the priceless past and of Ireland's ancient kings. Historic echoes are everywhere — in the splendid wood and stone carvings, handsome paneling, original oil paintings, and romantic walled garden.

All the pleasant accoutrements of luxurious comfort and convenience have been added with exquisite taste. Your room, such as those in Queen Anne Court, is charmingly furnished in a spirited color scheme, and overlooks a lovely flowered courtyard. The Queen Anne Court, which was built by Sir Edward O'Brien in 1736, is connected to the present main building by a carpeted corridor.

Your every comfort has been anticipated. Dining at Dromoland is divine and served in the classic continental manner, but Ireland's own specialties add zest to the cuisine. Try their Irish soda bread; it is a treat but different.

The staff has been well trained, and your dining here is as important to your attendants as it is to you. They are very jovial and want to please.

"*A fairyland setting for a golfing challenge*"

 Golfing at Dromoland is a great way to get off your jet lag if you have traveled from afar. It's only nine holes, but plenty of winding fairways, traps, and trees will add to your challenge. The rough is almost impossible and very easy to find.

This is the spectacular coast of County Clare and the golf course offers you pleasures in full measure. Remember there are no electric carts, but the exercise can be invaluable.

Tennis, fishing, and boating, plus shooting and deep sea fishing nearby offer alternate sporting fun.

I know now where the old saying, "Make hay while the sun shines," comes from. It was 9:30 p.m. as we left dinner to walk around the grounds, and the farmers were still cutting their hay. We were astounded, it was such a reality.

Dromoland extends a gracious welcome to all and will be proud to be your host. Be sure to check out their art as it is all museum quality.

Gleneagles Hotel

PERTHSHIRE, SCOTLAND

Gleneagles Hotel is more than a place to stay. It is a great hotel. Open all year round, this elegant Edwardian structure has played host to international guests for over 60 years. Years of enduring service and quality have brought Gleneagles a Five Star Hotel rating. Their philosophy is to insure each guest the utmost in service and attention. Graciousness and charm radiate throughout the spacious public areas, the intimate bars, and the grand dining rooms.

Accommodations range from guest bedrooms to suites. All are

comfortably decorated and many are being redone at this time.

The hotel's reputation owes much of its excellence to its cuisine. Scotland is blessed with great game, seafood, salmon, meat, and vegetables, and under the guidance of masters of classic French style cooking, such food has become their art.

The Main Dining Room insures attention and service and Continental fare to your perfect liking.

If you are a "gourmet," you will love dining in their Gourmet Room with a domestic and imported wine cellar unlimited.

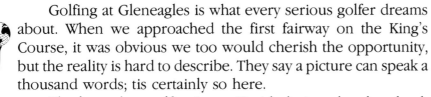 Golfing at Gleneagles is what every serious golfer dreams about. When we approached the first fairway on the King's Course, it was obvious we too would cherish the opportunity, but the reality is hard to describe. They say a picture can speak a thousand words; tis certainly so here.

The legendary golfer, James Braid, designed and took advantage of every slope, terrain, tree, and bush on this elegant property.

A Par 71, 6,503 yards long, this course really cuts your work out for you. It is a long course, but with its wide fairways, one can still score pretty well.

Gleneagles is not the typical seaside links but is manicured to perfection. Though they have a lot of play, since the course is so famous, still you feel as though you are playing at your own private country club. Their rolling fairways accented with flowers everywhere, trees, and Mother Nature in all her glory will assure you an everlasting memory of your golf in Scotland.

This is a favorite course among most of the world's golf professionals, and it was obvious to us why so many tournaments have been held here.

The Queen's Course is as beautiful but offers a different challenge and is said to be a "wee bit" less demanding.

The Prince's Course was opened as a nine-hole, but in 1974 was extended to 18 and has become a popular family course, geared for all levels of players.

The Glendeven Course brings even more variety for the enthusiast.

"Years of enduring service and quality"

Gleneagles is best known for golfing, but it is a sporting hotel in every sense. They offer squash, tennis, billiards, croquet, pony trekking and clay pigeon shooting, game and rough shooting, as well as salmon and trout fishing. A swim in their wonderful indoor pool, sauna, or massage could end your day in a completely perfect way.

The Hythe Imperial

KENT, ENGLAND

 Set in its own 52 acre estate with splendid sea views, the Hotel Imperial embodies impeccable standards and quiet elegance of a by-gone era with all the modern amenities. All the beautifully appointed bedrooms and suites are individually and thoughtfully furnished, giving them a gracious country house atmosphere. A choice of accommodations range from single, twin or double bedded rooms, 4-poster bed suites, and family suites.

Renowned for the excellent cuisine and fine wine cellar, you can plan on an exquisite gourmet experience. Their local seafood is freshly caught and served as their particular specialty.

If you are in a formal mood, the main dining room will be an event, and if your mood is for lighter fare or snacks, there are several areas including the hotel bar or leisure complex. If you want a private dining room, this can happen too.

A nine-hole 18 tee golf course is on the resort property and is situated among beautiful trees, sea views and as though this were not enough, Sene Valley is an 18-hole downland course where guests play at reduced fees. It is a par 67. Besides the golf course there is a putting green, tennis, on grass or all-weather courts, heated pool, sauna, sun beds, squash courts, table tennis, and a pool. There are also seven championship golf courses within 20 miles.

This beautiful seafront hotel is in Hythe, a charming Cinque Port town full of history, which has remained unspoiled. You will enjoy a warm welcome here with a personalized approach.

Racquetball courts, a beautiful health club plus indoor and outdoor swimming pools are all within this peaceful and quiet ocean-swept locale. If you elect to stay in one of the 300 1- and 2-bedroom villas, they are all luxurious. Elegant home rentals are available if you should want privacy.

La Forestière at Saint Germain

EN LAYE, FRANCE

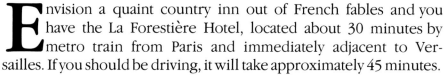

Envision a quaint country inn out of French fables and you have the La Forestière Hotel, located about 30 minutes by metro train from Paris and immediately adjacent to Versailles. If you should be driving, it will take approximately 45 minutes.

The Inn has 30 chambers and six apartments, all with radio, color television, and mini bars. Not particularly lavish, but comfortable and well decorated. This hotel is listed among the leading hotels of the world.

The food service is exquisite, and you could not want more. Attentive and pleasant, each of your attendants has been trained to please your most discriminating needs.

At the Cazaudehore Four-star restaurant, luncheons and dinners are often served in the gardens, in an atmosphere of pines and flowers. Colorful accents in fine linens accompanied by the perky flowered centerpieces complete a perfect setting.

The hotel is privately owned and it is obvious why this is a preferred spot in France. There are also two other quaint dining rooms for indoor dining during weather changes.

Close by is the picturesque Saint Germain Golf Club where you are playing in the middle of a forest. After the hectic pace of Paris, the fresh air plus the greenery and a most challenging championship golf course may be the greatest thing a traveling golfer could ask for. It's not uncommon to see deer here, as they roam freely.

Many undulating greens add to the interest and demand of this 6,115-yard course, and many characteristics of a Scottish course have been mingled in as well. Par is 72 for *messieurs* and 73 for *dames*.

On hole #17, you have to hit over shrubs, bushes, and trees with a small green to land on, and the effort can really bring you to your knees. Slices and hooks are "no no's" as every fairway is dotted with towering pines and bushes.

Many tournaments are hosted here, and though it is a private club, guests of the hotel can usually get a tee time. However, they do recommend booking ahead if you plan to play weekends.

Tennis is in full swing with numerous courts. Horses are nearby for riding.

If tranquility, peace and quiet are to your liking, you will enjoy the pace here.

*"A
country inn
out of
French
fable"*

Los Monteros

MARBELLA, SPAIN

Synonymous with quality and international prestige

Located in an exceptional setting of Marbella, Los Monteros is one of the renowned internationally known Five Star hotels. A perfect spot for rest and relaxation, it is a world of sport, too.

It is obvious when you enter the resort that care has been given to the most insignificant detail. Your concern and their personal attention is what this hotel is about.

The rooms are wonderfully comfortable and colorfully decorated, and offer all the amenities you would expect from a resort of this calibre. Walking to the rooms, you will find nature ever-present in this paradisiacal spot where the outside and inside worlds blend together perfectly—flowers, trees, ponds, waterfalls, etc.

Restaurant "Principal" table d'hote is a la carte. On the main floor, and at lunchtime or on the pool terrace, weather permitting.

Famous breakfasts are served free of charge to their guests.

Restaurant El Corzo's a la carte grill is on the ground floor of the Mirador from June 1st through September 30th.

Restaurant "La Cabane," an open air buffet, is casual enough to eat in your swimsuit.

The Golf Club coffee shop serves sandwiches and snacks as well as your favorite drinks.

Nightlife in the Pabellon Andaluz is always a special treat as you dance to and enjoy the beautiful Los Monteros orchestra.

Bar Azul, Hoyo 19, La Cabane, and Club De Tenis assure you of any liquid you may desire.

The "Rio Real" Golf Club, four kilometers from Marbella and two kilometers from the hotel, is a par 72 and is 6,130 meters. Beautifully landscaped and very well-groomed, it is enjoyed by an international clientele.

Rigid rules for guests assure you of a perfectly manicured course. A well-equipped pro shop provides rentals if necessary. A beautiful clubhouse and practice greens will add to your pleasure, plus changing rooms, showers and a coffee shop.

GRAN LUJO

They are famous for their riding club located at the foothills of the Sierra Blanca. "La Cabane" Beach Club has two magnificent pools, one heated indoor, with a restaurant and select buffet and bars. If you are a beachcomber, you will thrill at the wonderful beach.

A new, plush $20-million facility now sits less than a yard off a golf course that is the world's oldest and certainly one of the most distinguished to a golfer. Called the Old Course Golf and Country Club, this facility now can provide you with the luxury of a well decorated room, where careful plans were made to insure a world class golf traveler every comfort of home. Presently 80 bedrooms are complete, and that number will increase to 130.

The beautiful Eden Restaurant offers superior French food and is a favorite to many after a day on the links. Food is served with pride and in "grande" British style. British fare or wild game on the top floor at the Road Hole Carvery Grill is a good choice, too.

The Swilken Bar offers a magnificent vista of two golf courses

Old Course Hotel & Country Club

ST. ANDREWS, FIFE, SCOTLAND

and the North Sea beyond. At the 17th Hole on the ground level, you can observe other players' delight and frustration through smoked glass while still enjoying your food and drink.

The Road Hole lounge bar is conveniently located and promises to quench your thirst. The Jigger Inn, once a stationmaster's house, is still luring golfers in to discuss the doings of the day.

 Concerning those doings, St. Andrews offers plenty. The Scots originated and have nurtured the world's most popular game, and their expertise has helped produce courses in almost every country on earth. As Americans, we were especially interested to learn that in November of 1888, five expatriate Scots shipped equipment from the Tom Morris Golf Shop in St. Andrews to New York, where they created the first golf club our continent had ever seen, the St. Andrews Club at Yonkers.

The historic Old Course is almost indescribable. Surely this is one of the best known and best loved courses in the world because of its richness in golf history. A Par 72, it is 6,578 yards, but seems to play much longer. It is your extreme typical links course with parallel fairways. "One does have to be careful."

Many of the huge sloping and testy greens are shared by golfers from different holes which is sometimes confusing.

Part of the time you can plan on looking for your ball in their traditional rough, and many times you will come out empty-handed. Take plenty of balls with you.

If you are not a good sand player, here's a suggestion: practice before you get here.

Besides the Old Course, another playing pleasure awaits you on the sister course, the Eden, known to be just a "smidge" easier.

"A $20-million facility at the birthplace of golf"

Absorbing the atmosphere of this very special town is part of the excitement of golf here. There are fun, charm, and stimulating times ahead for you here in this town known everywhere as the HOME OF GOLF.

A world-renowned spa, claiming to have an ideal cure.

Quellenhof
BAD RAGAZ, SWITZERLAND

A resort of old standing and international reputation, this is one of Switzerland's leading golf and spa hotels. Completely renovated and modernized elegantly, this grand European hotel sits amidst large, quiet parks and beautiful gardens. The recently renovated rooms have been carefully decorated in a Continental style and offer every amenity, including phones and radios.

The large dining rooms are luxurious, and the food and service are in the European tradition.

Golf Club Bad Ragaz is a true gem nestled in the beautiful Swiss Alps, and is really one of the most scenic courses we have played. Besides the breathtaking view of the pine-studded Alps, everywhere you look the fairways are mingling and sloping into each other making a blanket of perfectly manicured greenery alive before your eyes.

Though Par is 70, it can play hard as there are some sloping fairways that even with your best shot roll out of sight.

Traps, many of them surrounding each green, also test your skill and chip shots. Beautiful birds, fish, flowers, and immaculate groundskeeping make this a course you will not only enjoy, but will always remember.

Claiming to have the ideal cure, this famous thermal spa is visited by people worldwide. Besides the thermal, they also have fresh water pools. Quellenhof is especially proud of their medical institute, which offers numerous special treatments and diets.

If you like to gamble, the Kursaal Casino is quite a place.

Be sure to stroll through the park. It is magnificent and just a five-minute walk to the quaint and small historical city of Bad Ragaz.

"One of the most scenic courses in the world"

Schlosshotel Kronberg

KRONBERG, GERMANY

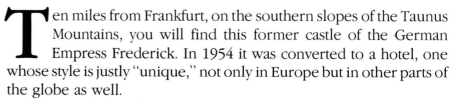

Ten miles from Frankfurt, on the southern slopes of the Taunus Mountains, you will find this former castle of the German Empress Frederick. In 1954 it was converted to a hotel, one whose style is justly "unique," not only in Europe but in other parts of the globe as well.

The castle hotel is open year round, its architecture being a mixture of various styles with English Tudor clearly prevailing.

Here, a guest never feels as though he is in a hotel. Private terraces offer beautiful views of an extensive park, and the magnificent trees and well-manicured golf course are certainly an eyeful.

The guest rooms are suites and are extravagantly decorated with antiques and period furniture; yet every amenity will await you, as will their cordial staff. Service is second nature to them, which is why they have many repeat guests, year after year.

Dining is available in the formal dining room or downstairs in a typical German restaurant, and the cuisine is excellent, conforming to the standards of a house with an international reputation.

"The former castle of the German Empress Frederick"

Golf amidst nature's splendor is a "happening" here. A championship course that is one of the most perfectly manicured anywhere will prove both challenging and interesting. All fairways slope into each other and makes for a most beautiful playground. Water, traps, and trees are always testy. Each hole is different and winds among the many flowers, pines, and other trees. This is no time or place for a slicer. The greens are true, but many are undulating, adding a need for your special touch. Though not a really tough course, it can be a great stop for a tune up, and a very worthwhile stopping off point when in West Germany. Par is 68 on this 5,365-meter course.

The combination of the castle and its history, wonderful accommodations, food service, and a beautiful golf course is a find you will enjoy knowing about.

T raveling in the footsteps of your ancestors can be a marvelously enriching experience, and on your arrival at this deluxe hotel, you will be taken back in time. Son Vida is a 13th century castle, complemented with fine antiques, charm, and comfort, and beautifully situated in a 1,400-acre private hilltop estate, yet is only minutes from the center of Palma. A most extraordinary hotel with a magnificent view of the Mediterranean Sea, Son Vida is a five-star *Grande Luxe* which beckons and pleases the most particular traveler.

Minutes after our arrival when the attendant met us at the door of this five-star hotel in the Balearic Islands, we felt assured that all our needs would be satisfied. Graceful and distinguished living was in evidence as we entered our room, facing the Palma Bay. The spaciousness was what attracted us to this room, not to mention the lovely decor and a million-dollar view. Rolling green fairways trailed down to the harbor, and we could spy the sea-going vessels along with the shimmering lights of the city below.

Service was a dream come true, and being so far from home, this was a refreshing experience.

Son Vida

PALMA DE MALLORCA

 The next morning, playing golf, we were again captured by Son Vida's scenic beauty. But the course was difficult to say the least. It's a championship course, and we felt like true "champs" when we were finished. This course is not to be taken lightly as it can really intimidate you.

Plenty of water, woods, shrubs, and flowers are there to greet you along with the up and down of a canyon terrain. Add to this some of the world's most beautiful scenery, and taking your eye off the ball could hardly be a misdemeanor.

The Par 3's were truly "grown up." We learned that Europeans make this a must on their list of golfing vacations, and once you have tried it, I feel sure it will be on yours.

Since we were at Son Vida a few years ago, there has been a change of owners and now the Sheraton Hotels have taken over with their tradition of excellence and attention to detail. You can't miss with this one-of-a-kind establishment.

Dining is exquisite and served in *grande* European elegance. Their international clientele adds extra excitement to the total atmosphere. Son Vida is known as "home away from home" to many globetrotters.

*"Old
castle
hotel with
'New World'
ideas"*

Turnberry
Hotel

AYRSHIRE, SOUTH WEST, SCOTLAND

A most popular resort for an experienced golfer or an amateur – sure to capture your attention with its charm.

Majestically this beautiful hotel sits perched on her hill with flags gently waving in the soft breezes, overlooking the blue waters of the sea and commanding a sweeping view of the golf courses as well.

On the Firth of Clyde with Ailsa Craig and the Isle of Arran just across the water, Turnberry was part of the Marquis of Ailsa's Culzean Estate. It began to flourish after the Marquis agreed to the develop-

ment of golfing facilities by the Glasgow and South Western Railway. By 1907 Turnberry had become a recognized golfing center with a first class hotel.

Situated amidst 360 acres of delightful Scottish countryside in the heart of South West Ayrshire, this internationally famous hotel can provide the ideal base to enjoy a traditional Scottish holiday.

Accommodations at the Turnberry Hotel are furnished in traditional style and all rooms meet the highest international standards. Each of their 124 bedrooms has color TV and private bath, and if you wish a suite, they have them, too.

For the dedicated golfer, they also have the Dormy House where after a day's play you may visit with other golf enthusiasts in the comfortable lounge. In this relaxed setting, other residents may relive their golf with you well into the night.

The Dormy House has its own private coffee shop, the Tappie Toorie, and Golfers Bar, with pleasing food and drink service. It is adjacent to the well-stocked and managed pro shop. You will also enjoy dining in the hotel's main dining room where food and service are impeccable. The dining room serves fresh fish, usually caught in local waters, as well as continental fare and dishes from the country.

Two internationally famous golf courses at this Four Star Hotel offer an open invitation to all golfers willing to accept their challenge.

The Ailsa recognizes no master, yet affords every golfer the same challenge and opportunity. The hallmarks of the Ailsa are known to all golfers who have played her.

MacKenzie Ross's subtle, deceptive use of Turnberry's natural beauty has created a links course which is a stern but fair test of any golfer's skill. A Par 71, it is 6,855 yards long. The Arran is a Par 69 measuring 6,276 yards. Being slightly shorter, it is considered a little less demanding than its sister course.

You can get in plenty of trouble here, as the links courses have rough that is unbelievable to deal with. On both of these courses, legendary players have enjoyed the sweet taste of success and the bitterness of defeat.

No matter how you score on either course, you will always savour your memories of this outstanding resort, as the views alone are captivating and some of the finest in the world.

Caddies are available as well as pull carts, or you may carry your own bag.

"Perched on a hill with flags gently waving, majestically she stands"

A sauna, gymnasium, solarium, swimming pool, and tennis room are added sports options. Don't miss some sightseeing in the area; the hotel will be most happy to arrange it for you.

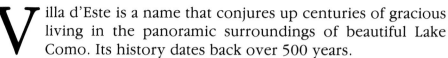

Villa d'Este

LAKE COMO, ITALY

Villa d'Este is a name that conjures up centuries of gracious living in the panoramic surroundings of beautiful Lake Como. Its history dates back over 500 years.

This stately hotel has been host to many presidents, kings, and dignitaries. Truly glamorous and extremely beautiful, it is a showcase you will not forget. The wonderful, ornate decor, including fine antiques and collectors paintings has been streamlined in order to provide up-to-date service; however, none of its old fashioned charm has been affected.

Guest rooms are individually designed, and no two are alike. The furnishings of elegant taste and beauty have preserved the impressive aura of its noble past. Each room has the intimacy of a private home.

The cuisine is prepared for a diversity of tastes and in various settings. The formal dining room and covered veranda offers sumptuous food in a romantic setting. The Grill with a rustic and informal milieu and in summer outdoor lunches and dinners are served in the garden. Totally charming...

For the younger set a lively discotheque. The nightclub is more formal, featuring a leading band, everyone has fun until the A.M.

The Canova room is always pleasant, with a pianist and entertainment for divertissment.

In 1926 the famous Villa d'Este 18-hole Championship Golf Course and Clubhouse were inaugurated at Montorfano. It is seven miles from the hotel and is considered one of the most challenging in the area. Located in a very attractive countryside, the championship course winds over slopes and valleys amidst luxurious woods along the charming lake at Montorfano with scenery similar to the north European countries. It is often referred to as a corner of Scotland.

Though it is private, Villa d'Este guests have playing privileges. There are also seven 18-hole courses in easy reach of the hotel by car.

A landmark is their unique floating swimming pool, literally floating on the lake. Other sporting attractions include all water sports from motorboating, canoeing, sailing and water-skiing to wind-surfing, monoskiing and sky skiing. Hang-gliding and parachuting are very popular. Tennis courts are hidden in the upper part of the marvelous 18th century park, along with a jogging trail with checkpoints.

Complete sauna, turkish baths, steam and massage rooms offer you a total package. Whether you are there for business or pleasure, their attentive staff guarantees a memorable stay.

*A heaven here on
earth*

Waterville Lake Hotel

WATERVILLE, IRELAND

This is a superb hotel set in luxurious seclusion. Located in a lovely corner of Ireland, it is told to music: the music of clear, bubbling mountain streams, of the rhythmic Atlantic, and of quiet, moody lakes.

The many characters from all over the world who have come to this enchanting place to play their parts as international travelers have made Waterville their own place to stay and play.

The hotel overlooks beautiful Lough Currane and complements its setting — an elegant spacious structure, luxuriously and tastefully appointed. The design affords breathtaking views from most areas.

Rooms consist of suites, apartments, and penthouse bedrooms and are colorfully but comfortably decorated. Food service is impeccable and the cuisine of continental or Irish tradition will be to your liking as they have enjoyed an international reputation for years. Served in their main dining room, you will be comfortable as you overlook the placid lake. If you elect your *aperitif* before dinner, you will enjoy cordiality in their unique bar or sitting room.

Waterville is elegant with a real touch of hominess. You do not feel as though you are in a hotel. The staff provides deluxe service, and the traditional Irish charm is, of course, complimentary.

The golf course is one of the largest championship links in Europe, measuring 7,118 yards, including tees stretching 175 yards. This is a links course set in an amphitheatre of mountains and fringing on the Atlantic shore. Farsighted designers took care to ensure that the beauty of the natural terrain was preserved, and today Waterville plays host to golfers from all over the world, seeking the challenge and the joy that is golf.

Besides the length, some fairways are incredibly narrow, making accurate shots a necessity. Numerous bunkers and lots of water can be trying as can the rough that identifies with a seaside link course.

You will be impressed with this course and also with the way it is maintained. A friendly reminder — take plenty of balls with you.

Tennis and swimming from wide, sandy beaches are available if you want a change.

It has been said that no one goes to Waterville just once. You may go there alone, but you will never be lonely.

The beauty of the natural terrain has been preserved on this famous links course.

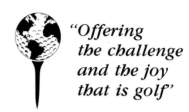

"Offering the challenge and the joy that is golf"

The grande dame of Mexico's resorts, this striking hotel dominates a site fronting Revolcadero Beach along the Pacific Ocean with the Sierra Madre Mountains as a backdrop. The moment you enter this 200-acre resort past lush green fairways dotted by lagoons and clusters of coconut palms, your excitement begins. Add to this the beauty of flowering acacias, monkeypod trees, and towering sculptured rock waterfalls.

The magnificent structure of the hotel is one continuous vertical sweep leading upwards past 16 bougainvillea-draped balconies. The 20,000-square-foot lobby is dramatic as is the spiral staircase descending from the first floor. Handcrafted Mayan columns, a palm-fringed lagoon, and accents of vibrant-colored, hand-woven fabrics create even more excitement.

Everywhere you look is another attention-getter. The El Grotto swim-up bar surrounded by tumbling waterfalls, flowers, and tropical palms plus the huge free-form pool is a showplace.

Seven hundred twenty-one rooms and suites have had the same careful attention to decor with each spacious guest room featuring a private terrace, air conditioning, radio, and direct dial telephone. Terrazzo floors, hand-carved mahogany furniture and doors, hand-woven fabrics in interesting color schemes, live plants, and original paintings complete the appointments.

The pyramid, or main building, houses 420 rooms, 41 suites, and six penthouses which are used by notables from time to time. Connected by a walkway is the 10-story tower building which houses 263 additional rooms. At the present time, yet another nearly identical tower is under construction.

Over six restaurants and five cocktail lounges are yours to choose from, offering a lot of variety during your stay.

There's something here for every taste and mood, whether it be French *haute cuisine* in their Holiday Award-winning Le Gourmet Restaurant to the Chula Vista with its unrivaled breakfast and dinner buffets.

Acapulco Princess

ACAPULCO, MEXICO

La Hacienda is another award-winning restaurant and is one of Acapulco's most popular dining spots. A converted Mexican hacienda, the restaurant features steaks from their own working cattle ranch. The main dining room offers continental fare in an atmosphere of comfortable elegance, while strolling musicians add a romantic touch to your evening. Cafe Poquito is open 24 hours, serving both American and Mexican specialties. Coco Loco nightclub stages typical Las Vegas revues and is loved by all.

 The 18-hole golf course, Par 72, is certainly championship calibre and was designed by golf architect Ted Robinson. Though only 6,400 yards long, it can be ever so tricky. The well-tended greens and the beauty surrounding it make it a delight for any golfer. The hazards come through the lagoons and coconut palms. Fairways are not so wide as to allow slicing or hooking. Beware…

You will enjoy the clubhouse as it offers a complete stock of golf equipment, and it is mandatory to use electric carts.

The Acapulco Princess' sister hotel is the neighboring Pierre Marques. It offers another 18-hole, Par 72 championship golf course which may be enjoyed by guests at both resorts.

For swimming and sunning, the beach is popular and extremely beautiful. Tennis buffs can find equal delight.

Shopping arcades are located in the Pyramid building and are stocked with everything from leather goods and hand-crafted items to art galleries and designer clothes.

An immense conference center and banquet rooms have made this property an ideal spot for meetings.

The Acapulco Princess lures visitors to its sandy shores 365 sunny days year-round. If you are looking for a sunny golfing vacation, you may have been lured.

Above, the magnificent structure of the hotel is a commanding presence of the Pacific shoreline.

 *"The grande dame of Mexico's resorts"*

A journey into the Hotel Las Hadas wonderland brings unexpected and unexcelled pleasures with a rich profusion of fragrant bougainvillea and a gentle surf rimmed in silky sand. This attractive $33-million Moorish wonderland commands favor and your attention. *Esquire* calls it "one of the eight most luxurious resorts in the world." A winding mosaic of cobblestones, cool gushing fountains, graceful archways, and picturesque plazas are vivid in your mind once you participate in it. It is like the end of the rainbow and the beginning of a dream.

Accommodations are sumptuous. Suites and rooms or villas in ornamental towers are all private with individual terraces overlooking the azure waters of Manzanillo Bay. All rooms have gleaming

marble floors, splendidly decorated with splashes of color. Access to every amenity imaginable, and some you never thought of, will make this visit exciting.

Dining anywhere in Las Hadas offers unique gourmet pleasures, with specialties to tantalize your taste buds. The elegant Legazpi, the *al fresco* Oasis, the charming Las Piñas all offer magnificent vistas and menus. To quaff your thirst, you can choose from seven enchanting bars.

At the exotic beach tent, Al Sarab serves spirited potions that automatically invite you to linger. Coco Loco and Cafe Doña Albina are two more sweet spots.

 Though the range of recreational pleasures is endless at Las Hadas, their golf course is finally one of the most lavish. Designed by renowned Roy Dye, it is rated 71 and measures 5,994 yards from the championship tees. The course is called La Mantarraya and got its name from the wonderful hole #18, because if the golfer does not reach the green, the ball disappears to be devoured by *"la mantarraya,"* the sting ray which inhabits Las Hadas Bay.

The renowned architect has said developing this course provided one of the biggest satisfactions for all who participated in it — but the challenge has really started since then.

Las Hadas
MANZANILLO, MEXICO

"A $33-million Moorish wonderland"

Recreational facilities begin with the main pool, which looks more like a lagoon. The iguanas love to eat hibiscus from your fingers but turn their snouts at any other flower. An authentic rope bridge spans the pool, and two exotic waterfalls add drama to this spectacular setting.

The private beach is 500 yards of golden sand and dotted with Moorish-style beach tents where a guest can seek respite from the sun or seek privacy with a friend.

Water sports, fishing, and cruising offer more fun, including excursions to Manzanillo for a sunset to remember. Tennis is another popular sport.

Internationally acclaimed and star-studded with "who's who's," Las Hadas can keep you happily enjoying.

Hotel do Frade

ANGRA DOS REIS, BRAZIL

"the best of Brazil"

Located in one of the most beautiful resorts on the Green Coast, about 2½ hours from Rio in a valley that ends at the sea, the "Hotel do Frade" mixes sophistication of a four star hotel and the pleasant easy-going life of the sea. There are 106 rooms, 11 suites, 16 bungalows and 79 bedrooms comfortable but delightfully decorated.

Two wonderful restaurants to serve you; whatever your liking may be found here. For a formal affair you will find fabulous food and candlelight dining amidst a spectacular seaside setting. For informal fun and fare you will enjoy western or food of the country. Delicious...and bars are a plenty, no need for thirst here.

At this writing the first nine golf holes are perfect, but nine more are in progress. Their goal is to be recognized as an International championship, first class golf course. Though very challenging, it is equally picturesque with several holes fronting the ocean. Plenty of water, sand and sea. The architects were Peter Allis and David Thomas.

The course is 6500 yards long and is very scenic.

Here simplicity goes with comfort, respecting nature as much as possible.

Wrapped by the sea breezes, amidst the sea of crystal waters and white sand, it is in a unique tropical setting...

As an amazing center for tourists, the hotel is equipped with a marina, five schooners, motor boats, etc. The leisure options are varied, from just plain sunbathing, on the hotel's private beach, water skiing, scuba etc...

In addition to all of this there is horseback riding, tennis, two swimming pools and saunas.

Sightseeing is very popular here and they have their own air conditioned buses to take you everywhere, including the Copacabana, and Iponema...

The Frade Hotels have for the past several years set the pace and standards for resort hotels in the area. Accompanied by comfort and care from their staff you will not be disappointed if you make it HOTEL do FRADE.

*Playing through the cycle of nature this green coast will
offer such pleasure and beauty you will wish the sun never sets.*

Pacific Harbour
International Resort

PACIFIC HARBOUR, FIJI

Everything you could possibly want from a golf holiday can be had here. Pacific Harbour is a quiet place, filled with natural beauty, swaying palms, and miles of golden beaches, plus every color and tropical flower imaginable.

Beautifully appointed rooms and suites with every possible amenity will welcome you. Your balcony will face the beautiful "Bega Island," one of the homes of the Fijian fire walkers. You may choose from a selection of fine villas too.

Catering to every taste in cuisine, one of the superb restaurants is the Nautilus, offering a choice of beautiful music played by local Fijian groups. Also, the golf and country club is close by and offers superb selections. The Sakura House Japanese Restaurant across the road is a good option and offers the best in Japanese cuisine. If you opt for international food, they have a splendid menu, too.

At the Cultural Centre you will love the "Ia Mai" restaurant.

If you're looking for a quiet place, filled with natural beauty, swaying palms, and miles of golden beaches, you have it here.

Your ultimate golfing experience can be here as you weave yourself through the jungle of glorious purple, red and yellow hibiscus and past tropical lagoons. An 18-hole par 72 championship course, it was designed by Robert Trent Jones, Jr., and is 6,908 yards long. This course was the venue for the 1978 ladies' and men's world cup teams championships.

They have played host to many international tournaments and international figures and professionals as well. The opinion is unanimous—"extremely beautiful and challenging," but enjoyable. For sure one of the most spectacular and different courses ever.

A superb playground on land as well as in the water, with unlimited other activities. Tennis, boating, snorkeling, sailing, horseback riding, volleyball, and, of course, enjoying the international cultural centre, a favorite pastime.

On the Fiji Coral Coast at Pacific Harbour, the past has been created along with their fascinating lifestyles of the island at the Cultural Centre. For fun, R & R and excitement, "they have it all together."

Directory

UNITED STATES RESORTS

Admiralty Resort
781 Walker Way
Port Ludlow, Washington 98365
206-437-2222

Alisal
Solvang, California 93463
805-688-6411

Amelia Island Plantation
Amelia Island, Florida 32034
904-261-6161, 800-874-6878

Americana Lake Geneva
Lake Geneva, Wisconsin 53147
414-248-8811, 800-228-3278

The Arizona Biltmore
24th. St. & Missouri
Phoenix, Arizona 85016
602-955-6600, 800-528-3696

The Balsams
Dixville Notch
New Hampshire 03576
603-255-3400

Boca Raton Hotel & Club
Boca Raton, Florida 33432
305-395-3000, 800-327-0101

The Boulders Resort
P.O. Box 2090
Carefree, Arizona 85377
602-488-9009

The Breakers
Palm Beach, Florida 33480
305-655-6611

The Broadmoor
Colorado Springs,
Colorado 80901
303-634-7711

Broadwater Beach Hotel
Biloxi, Mississippi 39533
601-388-2211, 800-647-3964

Callaway Gardens
Pine Mountain, Georgia 31822
404-663-2281, 800-241-0910

Camelback Inn Resort & Golf Club
5402 E. Lincoln Drive
Scottsdale, Arizona 85252
602-948-1700, 800-228-9290

The Cloister
Sea Island, Georgia 31561
912-638-3611, 800-841-3223

Colonial Williamsburg
Williamsburg Inn
P.O. Box B
Williamsburg, Virginia 23185
804-229-1000, 800-446-8956

Concord Resort Hotel
Kiamesha Lake, New York 12751
914-794-4000

Desert Inn & Country Club
Las Vegas, Nevada 89109
702-733-4444, 800-634-6906

The Diplomat
Hollywood By The Sea,
Florida 33022
305-457-8111, 800-223-7650

The Doral
4400 N. W. 87th Avenue
Miami, Florida 33178
305-592-2000, 800-327-6334

Eagle Ridge Inn & Resort
Box 777
Galena, Illinois 61036
815-777-2444

Fairfield Glade
P.O. Box 1500
Fairfield Glade, Tennessee 38555
615-484-7521, 800 251-6778

Furnace Creek Inn
Death Valley, California 92328
619-786-2345

The Greenbrier
White Sulphur Springs
West Virginia 24986
304-536-1110, 800-624-6070

Grenelefe
3200 State Road 546
Cypress Gardens, Florida 33844
813-422-7511, 800-237-9549

Grossinger's
Grossinger, New York 12734
914-292-5000, 800-431-6300

Grove Park Inn & Country Club
290 Macon Avenue
Asheville, North Carolina 28804
704-252-2711, 800-527-9299

High Hampton Inn & Country Club
Cashiers, North Carolina 28717
704-743-2411

The Homestead
Hot Springs, Virginia 24445
703-839-5500

Horseshoe Bay Country Club Resort
 Box 7766
Horseshoe Bay, Texas 78654
512-598-2511

Hotel Hershey & Country Club
Hershey, Pennsylvania 17033
717-533-2171

Hound Ears
Box 188
Blowing Rock, North Carolina 28605
704-963-4321

Hyatt Regency Grand Cypress
One Grand Cypress Blvd.
Orlando, Florida 32830
305-239-1234

Hyatt on Hilton Head
at Palmetto Dunes
P.O. Box 6167
Hilton Head Island
South Carolina 29938
803-785-1234

Inn of the Mountain Gods
P.O. Box 259
Mescalero, New Mexico 88340
505-257-5141, 800-545-9011

Innisbrook
P.O. Drawer 1088
Tarpon Springs, Florida 33589
813-937-3124, 800-237-0157

Inter-Continental Hotel
at Port Royal Resort
135 South Port Royal Drive
Hilton Head Island,
South Carolina 29928
803-681-4000, 800-327-0200

Keystone
Box 38
Keystone, Colorado 80435
303-468-2316

Kiawah
P.O. Box 12910
Charleston, South Carolina 29412
803-768-2121, 800-845-2471

La Costa
Carlsbad, California 92008
619-438-9111, 800-854-6565

La Quinta Hotel
P.O. Box 69
La Quinta, California 92553
619-564-4111, 800-854-1271

Lexington Marriott Resort
    Griffin Gate
1800 Newtown Pike
Lexington, Kentucky 40511
606-231-5100

The Lodge at Pebble Beach
Pebble Beach, California 93953
408-624-3811

Lodge of the Four Seasons
Lake Road HH
Lake Ozark, Missouri 65049
314-365-3001, 800-392-3461

Loews Ventana Canyon Resort
7000 E. Ventana Canyon Drive
Tucson, Arizona 85715-9990
602-299-7696

Longboat Key Club
301 Gulf of Mexico Drive
Longboat Key, Florida 33548
813-383-8821, 800-237-8821

Marriott's Grand Hotel
Point Clear, Alabama 36564
205-928-9201, 800-228-9290

Marriott's Tan-Tar-A
Osage Beach, Missouri 65065
314-348-3131, 800-228-9290

Mauna Kea
P.O. Box 218
Kamuela, Hawaii 96743
808-882-7222, 800-367-5246

Mauna Lani Bay Hotel
P.O. Box 4000
Kawaihae, Hawaii 96743
808-885-6622, 800-367-2323

Mission Inn Golf & Tennis Resort
Box 441
Howey-In-The-Hills
Florida 32737
800-874-9053

The Mount Washington
Bretton Woods,
New Hampshire 03575
603-278-1000, 800-258-0330

Myrtle Beach Hilton
Myrtle Beach, South Carolina 29577
803-449-7461

New Seabury
P.O. Box B
New Seabury, Maine 02649
617-477-9111

Olympia Resort & Spa
Oconomowoc, Wisconsin 53066
414-567-0311, 800-558-9573

Palm Beach Polo & Country Club
13198 Forest Hill Blvd.
Wellington, West Palm Beach
Florida 33411
305-793-1113, 800-327-4204

P.G.A. National Golf Club
    at the Sheraton Resort
400 Avenue of the Champions
Palm Beach Gardens
Florida 33410
305-627-2000, 800-325-3535

PineIsle
P.O. Drawer 545
Lake Lanier Islands
Buford, Georgia 30518
404-945-8921, 800-323-4455

Pinehurst Hotel & Country Club
Pinehurst, North Carolina 28374
919-295-6811, 800-334-9560

Rancho Bernardo Inn
17550 Bernardo Oaks Drive
San Diego, California 92128
619-487-1611

Rancho de los Caballeros
Wickenburg, Arizona 85358
602-684-5484

The Resort Spa at Tucson
National Golf Club
8300 North Club Drive
Tucson, Arizona 85741
602-297-2271, 800-528-4856

Salishan Lodge
Glenedin Beach, Oregon 97388
503-764-2371

Samoset
Box 188
Rockport, Maine 04856
207-594-2511, 800-341-1650

Sawgrass
P.O. Box 600
Ponte Vedra Beach, Florida 32082
904-285-2261, 800-874-7547

Sea Pines Plantation
Hilton Head Island
South Carolina 29928
803-785-3333

Sheraton Molokai
Kepuhi Beach, Molokai, Hawaii 96770
808-552-2555, 800-325-3535

Sheraton Savannah Inn
& Country Club
612 Wilmington Island Road
Savannah, Georgia 31410
912-897-1612, 800-325-3535

Sheraton Tucson El Conquistador
10000 North Oracle Road
Tucson, Arizona 85704
602-742-7000, 800-325-3535

Shipyard Plantation
P.O. Box 7000
Hilton Head Island
South Carolina 29938
800-845-6135

Silverado
1600 Atlas Peak Road
Napa Valley, California 94558
707-255-2970, 800-227-4700

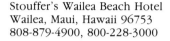

Stouffer's Wailea Beach Hotel
Wailea, Maui, Hawaii 96753
808-879-4900, 800-228-3000

Sugarloaf/USA
Kingfield, Maine 04947
207-237-2000

Sun Valley Lodge
Sun Valley, Idaho 83353
208-622-4111, 800-635-8261

Sunriver
Sunriver, Oregon 97702
503-593-1221, 800-547-3922

Tamarron
P.O. Drawer 3131
Durango, Colorado 81301
303-247-8801, 800-525-5420

The Tides Inn
Irvington, Virginia 22480
(804) 438-5000 (800) 446-9981

The Tides Lodge
Irvington, Virginia 22480
804-438-6000, 800-446-5660

Turnberry Isle Yacht & Country Club
19735 Turnberry Way
Miami, Florida 33180
800-327-7028, 305-932-6200

Walden on Lake Conroe
14001 Walden Road
Montgomery, Texas 77356
409-582-6441

The Wigwam
Litchfield Park, Arizona 85340
602-935-3811, 800-421-4000

Woodlands Inn & Country Club
2301 Millbend Drive
Woodlands, Texas 77380
713-367-1100

Woodstock Inn & Resort
14 The Green
Woodstock, Vermont 05091
802-457-1100, 800-223-7637

The World of Palm-Aire
2501 Palm-Aire Drive North
Pompano Beach,
Florida 33060
305-972-3300, 800-327-4960

INTERNATIONAL RESORTS

Acapulco Princess
P.O. Box 1351
Acapulco, Guerrero, Mexico

Ashford Castle
Cong, County Mayo,
Ireland

Atlantik Beach Hotel
P.O. Box F-531
Freeport/Lucaya,Bahamas

Bali Handara Country Club
Pancasari, Bali, Indonesia

Bali Hyatt
P.O. Box 392
Sanur, Bali, Indonesia

Banff Springs Hotel
Banff, Alberta, Canada
TOL OCO

The Belfry
Wishaw North Warwickshire
England B769PR
0675-70301

Brenner's Park-Hotel
An der Lichtenthaler Allee 7570
Baden-Baden,
West Germany

Britannia
West Bay Road
Grand Cayman, British West Indies

Burgenstock Estate
C H 6366 Burgenstock
Switzerland

Casa de Campo
La Romana
Dominican Republic

Cerromar Beach Hotel
Dorado
Puerto Rico 00646

Chung Shan Hot Spring Golf Club
Sanxiang Commune,
Zhongshan City
Guangdong Province, China

Cotton Bay Club
Rock Sound
Eleuthera
Bahamas

Discovery Bay Golf Club
Valley Road, Discovery Bay
Lantau Island, Hong Kong

Dolder Grand
Kurhausstrasse 65
8032 Zurich
Switzerland

Dona Filipa Hotel
Vale do Lobo
Almansil 8106 Loule Codex
Algarve
Portugal

Dorado Beach Hotel
Dorado
Puerto Rico 00646

Dromoland Castle
Newmarket-on-Fergus
County Clare
Ireland

Gentling Highlands
Kuala Lumpur, 06-24
Malaysia

Gleneagles Hotel
Perthshire
Scotland
   or
BTH Hotels, Inc.
185 Madison Avenue
New York, New York 10016

Gray Rocks
Mount Tremblant
C.P. 1000
St. Jovite, Quebec, Canada
JOT 2HO

Hakone Prince Hotel
144 Motohakone
Kanagawa 250-05
Japan

Hotel do Frade
Rua Joaquim Nabucco 161
San Jose, Brazil

Hyatt Central Plaza Bangkok
1695 Phaholyothin Road
Bangkhen, Bangkok 10900
Thailand

The Hythe Imperial
Hythe, Kent CT21 6AE
England

Jasper Lodge
P.O. Box 40
Jasper, Alberta
Canada TOE 1EO

Karuizawa Prince Hotel
1016-75 Karuizawa
Karuizawa-Machi
Kita-Saku-Gun
Nagano, Prefecture
Japan
389-01

Kawana Hotel
1459, Kawana Ito
Shizouka Prefecture
Japan

La Forestiere at Saint Germain
78100 Foret de Saint-Germain-en-laye
France

Las Hadas
Manzanillo, Colima
Mexico

Los Monteros
Marbella, Spain

Mahogany Run
Box 7517
St. Thomas, U.S.
Virgin Islands 00801

Marriott's Castle Harbour Resort
P.O. Box 841
Hamilton 5, Bermuda
(809) 293-8161

Old Course Hotel and Country Club
St. Andrews, Fife
Scotland KY 16 9SP

Pacific Harbour International Resort
Postal Agency
Pacific Harbour, Fiji 45011

Puerto Azul Beach Hotel Resort
Ternate, Cavite
Philippines

Quellenhof
7310 Bad Ragaz
Switzerland

Saint Geran
P.O. Box 56
Port Louis, Mauritius

Schlosshotel Kronberg
Hainstrasse 25
Postfach 1326
6242 Kronberg
West Germany

Son Vida
Palma de Mallorca 13
Spain

Sun City
Bophuthatswana
P.O. Box 5087
Johannesburg
South Africa

Tryall
Sandy Bay Post Office
Hanover
Jamaica

Turnberry Hotel
Ayrshire, Strathclyde
Scotland KA 26 9LT

Villa d'Este
Via Regina 40
22010 Cernobbio,
Lake Como, Italy

Waterville Lake Hotel
Waterville, County Kerry
Ireland

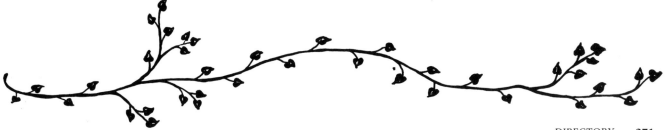